Dr Tom Harrison is a Reader in the School of Education at the University of Birmingham. He is the Director of Education for the Jubilee Centre for Character and Virtues. Tom's specialist interests are character education and virtue ethics, character, wisdom and the Internet, youth social action, and citizenship education. He has published extensively in these areas as well as developing resources and training programmes for schools, voluntary sector and other organisations. Tom currently leads the Masters in Character Education – a three-year distance learning degree. He is also a National Teaching Fellow, Trustee and Secretary for the Society for Educational Studies (SES) and Secretary and Trustee for the Association for Character Education (ACE). Tom has also co-authored the following books: *Educating Character Through Stories*; *Teaching Character in Primary Schools*; *Teaching Character and Virtue in Schools*; and *The Theory and Practice of Virtue Education* (edited collection).

Praise for *Thrive*

'Every parent is nervous about how their child will cope with the online world. Based on his work on building character and a desire for every child to flourish, Tom Harrison is just the right person to show us how the next generation can navigate cyberspace and thrive in doing so'
— The Rt Hon Baroness Nicky Morgan

'In the fourth industrial revolution, it is vital our children develop the character and human strengths that will enable them to flourish online. This book makes a compelling case for why character matters, as well as clearly showing how parents and teachers can help their children to use digital technologies wisely'
— Sir Anthony Seldon

'As a parent, I know how important it is to help young people flourish in the increasingly digital world in which they're growing up. In his new book, Tom Harrison shows us how the theory of character development – which can be traced back to the ancients – is more relevant to this task than ever. The book provides a practical guide for parents and young people on how to develop the wisdom and skills needed to navigate the internet, with all the opportunities and risks it provides. I highly recommend this book to all parents and teachers'
— Lord O'Shaughnessy

'While guides to keeping children safe on the internet abound, children deserve more – they deserve to flourish in the online spaces that form part of everyday life in the twenty-first century. Tom Harrison's *THRIVE* is a much-needed guide for parents, teachers and others seeking to help children cultivate the habits, virtues and practical judgment needed to live wisely and well in digital environments'
— Professor Shannon Vallor, Baillie Gifford Chair in the Ethics of Data and Artificial Intelligence

'*THRIVE* seamlessly weaves together timely insights from research on digital life, timeless ethical principles and actionable advice to help parents guide their children on the path to cyber-wisdom and, ultimately, to thrive. Tom Harrison draws from his own experiences raising children in a connected world and his deep expertise in virtue ethics and character education to create a compelling "how to" guide for parents'
— Dr Carrie James, Principal Investigator at Project Zero, Harvard Graduate School of Education

'*THRIVE* demonstrates the need for parents and teachers to take an active part in helping children to develop into good "cyber-citizens". The Internet offers temptations to a new generation that their parents and teachers may not have encountered. This sentence stayed with me: "Many children I interviewed said they had been involved with saying nasty things to others online because their friends encouraged them to." That's how easy it can be. Fortunately, Dr Harrison's work offers us strong and positive ways to "reclaim the language of virtue"'
— Naomi Stadlen, author of *What Mothers Learn*

'*THRIVE* is practical, realistic and sound. Tom Harrison's ideas resonate with my own experiences as a mother and educator of adolescents, and his parenting tools will be as effective in everyday life as in the digital world. Your child will thank you for reading this'
— Kim McCabe, founder of Rites for Girls and author of *From Daughter to Woman*

'Finally, a practical guide that not only tells us why our kids need to learn to become good cyber-citizens, but actually gives us the tools for how to do it! In two easy-to-remember acronyms, REACT and THRIVE, Tom empowers parents to enter our children's cyber worlds with proactivity and positivity rather than fear and negativity. He shows us how we can practically foster the wisdom in our kids that is so necessary in making good decisions in the cyber world on their own. This book is extremely relevant and I highly recommend it for parents and teachers'
— Jessica Joelle Alexander, bestselling author of *The Danish Way of Parenting*

THRIVE

How to
cultivate character
so your children
can flourish online

DR TOM HARRISON

A How To Book

ROBINSON

ROBINSON

First published in Great Britain in 2021
by Robinson

10 9 8 7 6 5 4 3 2 1

A CIP catalogue record for this book
is available from the British Library.

ISBN: 978-1-47214-473-7

Typeset in Sentinel and Scala Sans
by Ian Hughes

Printed and bound in Great Britain
by Clays Ltd, Elcograf S.p.A.

Papers used by Robinson are from well-
managed forests and other responsible
sources.

MIX
Paper from
responsible sources
FSC® C104740

Robinson
An imprint of
Little, Brown Book Group
Carmelite House
50 Victoria Embankment
London EC4Y 0DZ

An Hachette UK Company
www.hachette.co.uk

www.littlebrown.co.uk

How To Books are published by
Robinson, an imprint of Little, Brown
Book Group. We welcome proposals
from authors who have first-hand
experience of their subjects. Please set
out the aims of your book, its target
market and its suggested contents in
an email to howto@littlebrown.co.uk.

To Emma, Isla and Sam

Contents

Preface

Letting go

I bought my eleven-year-old daughter her first smartphone today; she has entered the cyber-world. It feels like a rite of passage, albeit a very twenty-first-century one. She is using the phone right now in the room next door, and I am nervous and proud. I am nervous because I used to worry about where she was when she left the house; now I worry about where she might be when she is in her bedroom. But I am also proud. Proud that I have a daughter whom I trust enough to hand such a powerful tool to. I know that the time is right for my daughter to have the phone. I trust her. Yet, I am still nervous.

This is what this book is about. It is my attempt, as a parent, to calm my nerves, through knowledge and understanding about the world my daughter is entering. Several years ago, I completed a PhD on the influence of the Internet on eleven- to fourteen-year-olds. As an academic, I have continued to research the field.[1] By most people's reckoning, this makes me an expert on the subject. Yet before I started this book, I felt like I knew nothing. This is because, although I had interviewed hundreds of children and read the work of the foremost experts in the field, my knowledge felt overly theoretical. I was good at telling other people what to do, but this was different. This time it is my daughter who has a phone; it feels more personal and more real. I need to arm myself with solid, hard, practical advice.

I don't need to know what to *think* any more, I need to know what to *do*.

Reacting and thriving

This desire for practical advice was the start of the journey of writing this book. It felt like a familiar journey as I retraced many of the steps I had previously taken in my research. This background provided the theoretical foundations for the arguments that I make. As I went back over this ground, I looked at my own and other people's research differently, through the eyes of a parent rather than an academic. I wanted to understand what the words on the page meant in the real worlds of my children and their friends.

I gathered evidence, ideas, theories and practical advice, and have combined them into two models. These models that you will be introduced to, REACT and THRIVE, are underpinned by the theory that I started developing during my early research. I have been honing these models ever since. It is the use of character education as the underpinning theory for these practical models that marks this book out from most others.

The book is ultimately about my role and responsibilities as a parent and what I need to do to help my daughter and son to live flourishing lives in their cyber-worlds. It is to help me to help them become wiser cyber-citizens.

I hope that you can also learn something from my journey.

The journey from rules for surviving to character for thriving

From the outset I want to sketch out briefly the core argument upon which this book rests. I am doing this for three reasons. First, you need to know this to make sense of everything that follows. Second, it is this core argument that makes this book different from others that have come before. Third, I hope you will be convinced about the approach I set out and want to read on and find out how to put the theory into practice.

What I am proposing is that the key to educating for cyber-wisdom and cyber-citizenship today lies in ancient wisdom, in a theory of character development that is more than two thousand years old. It might sound far-fetched, but the following arguments will convince you it is not.

Moral theories explain why acting in certain ways is right or wrong. In the West there are three major moral theories that shape pretty much our entire understanding of ethics and morality: deontology, utilitarianism and virtue ethics. For hundreds of years the first two of these have been in the ascendency.

Deontological philosophy is based on the moral principle that it is one's duty to follow rules and guidelines. This philosophy is most commonly associated with the philosopher Immanuel Kant.[2] If I was to follow a deontological strategy to manage my children's use of the Internet, I would restrict their access to their smartphones or tell them what games they can or cannot play. If we think of moral motivation in terms of carrots and sticks, this approach is the *sticks*.

Utilitarian philosophy is based on the principle that the 'right thing to do' is the action that brings the greatest happiness for the greatest number of people. It is a philosophy most commonly associated with Jeremy Bentham and John Stuart Mill.[3] If I was to follow a utilitarian strategy to manage my children's use of the Internet, I would focus their attention on their digital actions and try to get them to weigh up what the consequences of them might be. I might do this by showing them stories about young people who committed suicide after being cyber-bullied or by encouraging my children to think about what they write online and how this might be interpreted now and in the future. I could also try to implement a reward system to encourage my children to interact with their smartphones in the way I want them to. The approach is more about using *carrots* than sticks.

In dealing with issues such as sexting, trolling, cyber-bullying and other similar concerns, many of us turn to deontological or utilitarian strategies, or both. They can provide effective tools to manage Internet use. Although useful, they are insufficient on their own. This is because they don't seek to help our children self-manage their own Internet use. One day they are going to have to do this on their own – when we are not there to uphold rules or show them the possible consequences of their actions.

We have to prepare our children for the time when they have to go it alone.

There is another problem.

The freedom and affordances the Internet offers our children make it challenging to implement rules- and consequence-based strategies. This is because in the cyber-worlds that our children inhabit, rules are hard to establish and uphold, and consequences are difficult to predict. Rules may work in the classroom, but they are much harder to enforce in the chatroom. Parents can help their children see the consequences of how they communicate face to face with their siblings or friends, but they find it harder to help their children understand that a message or picture they send online could be hurtful. This is why children might behave differently online: they might bully online, but not face to face; they might plagiarise from a website, but not from a book; they might download an album illegally online, but not steal a CD from a shop.[4]

There is a third problem.

To be able to successfully adopt a rules- or consequence-based approach assumes we know what the future holds. With technology changing so rapidly, no one knows what is to come – so how can we make rules that will work in the future or predict consequences accurately? We don't know where robotics, AI, the Internet of Things, bioengineered humans and a great many other technological innovations on the horizon will take us. We don't know what effect they will have on society and humans. Some have tried to predict the effects. For example, before his death Stephen Hawking said that unrestricted AI could end the human race. But none of us can truly know the moral issues that technologies require us to grapple with in the future.

When rules- and consequence-based strategies are not working, we need to look for another way.

The third way

The moral theory that best equips us to deal with an uncertain future is virtue ethics. Virtue ethics is a theory that originates in the ancient Greek philosophy of Aristotle. His argument was that if we want to help people to do the right thing, then we have to educate them in character and virtue.

I apply the basics of a virtue-ethical argument in this book as follows:

We can try to apply rules and consequence-based educational strategies to help our children *survive* in the cyber-world. We need to apply character-based educational strategies if we want them to *thrive*.

This means we need to help our children cultivate character and cyber-wisdom – the human qualities associated with cyber-flourishing. In this book I will show you what this means and how to do this.

Why character matters

The educational approach I will outline in this book does not reject carrots-and-sticks parenting methods outright, but seeks to bolster them with an unrelenting focus on the cultivation of qualities in our children that help them to understand what the 'right' action is in any given online interaction.

It is not always obvious what the 'right' thing to do is in the many online situations our children face. This is why we need our children to develop qualities such as compassion, honesty, integrity and many others, but also, and most importantly, cyber-wisdom. I define cyber-wisdom[5] as: doing the right thing for the right reasons when online. This is a quality that children can apply in any given situation.

Character and cyber-wisdom take time to develop. We can help our children cultivate these essential human qualities over time, through experimentation; through getting things wrong and learning from them; through getting things right and celebrating them; through love, understanding and support; through encouraging personal reflection that ensures a maturing critical discernment.

The aim is that through thoughtful parenting the essential character qualities required to flourish online eventually become habits.

Character: a reawakening

Character is undergoing a resurgence. Individuals and organisations from all walks of life are (re)awakening to the power and importance of character. Here are a few examples:

- Since 2019 all schools in England have been inspected on their character-education provision. Schools can't get a good or outstanding rating on the new Ofsted framework unless they show how they are developing the character of their students. This was not the case previously.[6]

- Businesses have turned to theories of character since the financial crash in 2008. Although codes of conduct existed before the crash, they did not stop some bankers playing fast and loose with our money. Some people working in the financial sector were found to lack the character virtues of honesty and integrity, among others. In response, virtue ethics and character are becoming central to discussions about how to manage the ethical conduct of professionals.

- One of the reasons Gareth Southgate says the England football team got to the semi-finals of the 2018 World Cup was because of their individual and team character. He says England had skilful players in the past, but now England has skilful players who are able to show the character qualities required to play as a team.[7] It is not uncommon to hear managers and coaches talk about the importance of character in sport. For example, Jurgen Klopp – the boss of Liverpool FC – argues, 'In the Premier League, tell me one player who is not skilled. You mix that with the right character and now we can start talking about the right things.'[8]

- There is growing evidence, largely from the discipline of positive psychology, of the link between character and mental health. Evidence shows that the development of character strengths such as resilience, gratitude, courage, temperance and many others improves mental health. These discoveries are forming the foundation of virtue-based psychotherapeutic interventions. This is an interesting movement given that many children and young people today suffer from poor mental health, and some of this rise has been blamed on new technologies.[9]

- In a government-commissioned report about how to respond to the riots in England in 2011, character education was the main recommendation. Today, the Department for Education has a specialist team working on character and it is seen as one of the Department's priority areas. They make links between character education and other educational concerns such as attainment, wellbeing, mental health and employment.

- During the worldwide protests that sought to address systemic racism following the death of George Floyd at the hands of police, there were renewed calls for people to be judged on the content of their character rather than the colour of their skin.[10] The calls echo the words spoken by Martin Luther King Jr in his famous 'I Have a Dream' speech. Martin Luther King Jr believed, 'Intelligence plus character, that is the true goal of education.'[11]

I could give you plenty of other examples that demonstrate the resurgence of character in policy, education, business, parenting and elsewhere. We are waking up to the importance of character for individual and wider societal flourishing. We are reconsidering the merits of virtue ethics as a philosophy.

This is the first practical book in the UK to show parents and teachers how to apply virtue-ethical theory to help their children truly flourish online.

Structure of the book

This book is intended to be practical, but is grounded in theory and research. You will notice some sections of the book describe in detail the character-based theoretical underpinning that my arguments rest upon. This is deliberate, as I want you to understand what a character-based approach to developing and honing cyber-wisdom looks like. I also think these more theoretical sections serve a practical purpose. Good theory should do a number of things. It should bring you confidence in my approach, it should inform you about recommended actions and it should inspire you to take them. Of course, no one ever lives up to pure ideal theory – we are all too human and life is too messy for that. However, I believe the more theoretical sections of the book should provide you with some pointers for better parenting.

The book is also full of practical advice. You will learn that character is both caught and taught – and on balance mostly caught. To develop desirable character qualities including cyber-wisdom in your children, you can't follow a taught course. It is more about being aware of how you display character day to day and making adjustments if necessary. This is why the bulk of the book describes the types of parents and educators we need to be or become, as well as the qualities our children must develop and hone.

At the end of the book I provide an educational framework and suggested teaching activities for developing cyber-wisdom. Running these activities with your children will not guarantee to make them cyber-wise, but the activities will provide them with some important knowledge and tools that will enable them to move towards developing this quality independently and critically.

The book covers the following:

Part One makes the case for *why* we should care about how we educate our children in the age of the Internet and explains my approach, supported by evidence, to show *what* we have to do.

Part Two details the five components of the REACT model – the qualities that we adults must attend to. The components are: be a rule-maker, be an exemplar, be an advisor, be a character champion and focus on developing the qualities of the THRIVE model in children.

Part Three details the six components of the THRIVE model – the qualities our children must develop if they are to flourish online. These components are: be thoughtful, be human, be reasonABLE, have integrity, be virtuous and be an exemplar.

Part Four explains how cyber-wisdom can be developed through character education. It explains what character education is, details some of the key pedagogical approaches and finishes with a framework and associated activities for educating cyber-wisdom.

Being human

I am finishing up writing this book in the middle of the coronavirus global pandemic lockdown. When the crisis is over, I can see us looking back at the Internet as the technology that saved thousands of lives and reduced the impact on the economy. It has allowed scientists and doctors around the world to collaborate more easily as they search for a vaccine. It has enabled many people to continue working at home. It has helped many parents to continue to provide an education for their children when the schools closed. It has provided us with ways to connect with friends and family when we can't meet up with them. It has been a way that people can reach out to those in their community to ask for help getting food and medicines. It has been a much-needed source of entertainment. In many ways it has been an unsung hero during the pandemic.

The crisis has shown that when people with good character and wisdom use the Internet, it can truly enhance human flourishing around the globe.

As the outbreak spreads, I am reminded about the many positives of the Internet. Others have complained that too much that is written about the effects of the Internet on children is negative. I largely agree, but I also understand why. I am concerned about what my smartphone is doing to myself, let alone my children. I think it is therefore best to be positive and realistic – to see the opportunities and the risks.

To be positive and realistic requires a delicate balance. I don't want this book to contribute to a moral panic around cyber-technologies. Moral panics don't help us parent, as they are not subtle, nuanced or representative of the day-to-day experiences of most of us. They tend to frame everything in the negative and don't look closely at what is really going on. They start with a premise that, because a technology exists, a certain outcome is inevitable. This argument, for me, is overly deterministic. It denies the fact that we humans make and use the technologies. It is in our gift how we behave collectively to one another when we are online.

Writing this book has hopefully made me a better parent in the digital age.

I hope that it also helps you in some of the same ways.

Part One

Flourishing Online

1
Taking Back Control of Our Cyber-worlds

Losing control

I like order. I like knowing what is going on and what is going to happen. Cyber-technologies are marketed on the premise they help us to maintain order in our hectic lives: they ping us when we are late for a meeting; talk to us as we leave the house to remind us we need an umbrella; choose songs to play that they know (or think they know) we will like; allow us to work any place, anytime; tell us where our children are. They provide an illusion that they make our lives easier. The Big Tech marketing people would rather we did not question this illusion. They do not want us to ask if the Internet has actually made our lives more complex, more chaotic.

By falling for the illusion that the Internet can make our lives more ordered, we are also losing control. This is the concern I have.

This is not science fiction, this is not about AI or the robots taking over. Many books and films have already covered this in more or less dramatic ways. My concern feels more pernicious and perhaps less tangible. It is linked to a fear of individuals leading unhappy lives and societies languishing. My concern is that we are surrendering to cyber-technologies, losing our minds and our hearts to them.

We are sleepwalking into this situation. We have stopped thinking as we have forgotten our own humanity, our own agency – we are becoming technologically deterministic.

Who is in charge, technology or us?

The term technology determinism is used in various ways to describe how technologies *forcibly* shape people and societies. Extreme advocates of this view argue that we are powerless in the wake of technological progress, since by its very design it dictates users' behaviours and consequently diminishes human agency. This viewpoint is summed up by a belief that the machines are taking over and we are powerless to stop them.

I am not proposing anything so dramatic here. My concern, addressed in this book, is more prosaic, more mundane, but perhaps no less frightening. I believe that grand theories that pitch digital technologies against humans are unhelpful. We should not be tricked into a trap of describing emerging technologies in essentialist or absolute terms. Just because x exists, y does not have to happen. Just because my daughter has a mobile phone does not mean she will become a troll, a bully or start 'stealing' online content. This is a line of argument that is behind some of the more sensationalist media stories.

Technology is, after all, only as good (or bad) as the people who make or use it.

We hear that social media causes trolling, email makes us more stressed, that video games are addictive. Although all these things *might* be true to some extent, they do not *have* to be true. Social media could also increase goodwill, sharing and charitable giving; email could make friendly and kind exchanges more likely; and playing video games could increase our social and emotional skills. The same technologies with different outcomes.

There are features of new technologies that make us use them in ways that are sometimes unhelpful to ourselves and others.[1] But these very same features also mean we can connect and reach out to people for positive reasons, undertake actions that change lives and use the Internet to make a transformative difference.

The key point is that can we choose how we use the Internet. We can choose how to behave in the cyber-world just as we choose how to behave in the 'real' world. We make the technologies and we should be in control of how we use them – even if this is not easy and requires a great deal of self-discipline. This means it is our values, our character and our wisdom that ultimately matter.

We need to remind ourselves of this fact and communicate it to our children.

Leaving it to others

Why have so many of us seemingly forgotten that we are in control?

I think it is partly because we are not strong enough to resist the pull of the technologies and partly because we hope others will make the difficult decisions for us. On both counts we have stopped thinking.

It is easier for us to hope that the government or the makers of digital technologies will do the hard thinking for us. Our blind hope is that governments will step in to help us when needed or that technology companies have our best interests at heart. We trust them to regulate in our interests. This is largely a fantasy.

Big Tech will fight hard not to be regulated by governments; their business models depend on it. Most will do anything they can to maintain their freedom so that they can grow and, in doing so, gain ever-increasing amounts of our attention, which then translates into profits. Famously, the original Google slogan was 'Don't be evil',[2] but they did little in the way of active self-regulation to realise this vision. Mark Zuckerberg, the founder of Facebook, has stated on numerous occasions that he wants his platform to be a force for good. Although Facebook has been a tool used for good by many, it has also been used for purposes most of us would consider immoral. For example, Instagram (owned by Facebook) has been unable to identify and take down all self-harm content after it pledged to do so following the suicide of Molly Russell, a fourteen-year-old British schoolgirl, in 2017. Facebook has not exactly been rushing to take responsibility for this, although it does feel, most likely due to market forces, that things are starting to change. For example, between April and September 2019 the company removed 1.7 million images relating to suicide and self-harm.[3]

The billion-dollar question is – is it too late to turn around the tanker?[4]

A cynic might say that Facebook now claims it wants to regulate itself – something most companies would actively try to resist – as it realises it might start losing customers if it doesn't. Governments are starting to make louder noises about regulation. Again, although this sounds good, it is largely in the realm of fantasy. To date, governments have been found to be relatively powerless when it comes to bringing in meaningful regulation. For example, in 2019 the UK government had to drop its plans to implement the so-called porn block. The porn block was intended to make all under-eighteen-year-olds prove they were old enough before they could access websites with adult content. The Department of Culture, Media and Sport (DCMS) could not, due to practical reasons and lobbying from some companies, make the block work.

There are signs that the situation is changing, that governments are trying to get tougher and impose more rules on tech companies. For example, in 2019 the UK government carried out a consultation into online harms, which received 2,500 responses. One result of this consultation is that the regulator Ofcom will be given new powers to ensure social media companies protect people from harmful content, including violence, bullying, terrorism and child abuse. It has been suggested that companies will be liable for hefty fines if they don't take steps to protect children. This follows similar moves in other countries. For example, the NetzDG Law in Germany states that social media platforms with more than two million registered German users have to review and remove illegal content within twenty-four hours of it being posted or face fines that could be in the millions of Euros. Likewise, in Australia the Sharing of Abhorrent Violent Material Act introduced criminal penalties for social media companies that don't take steps to protect people from harmful content. The penalties include possible jail sentences for tech executives of up to three years and financial penalties worth up to 10 per cent of a company's global turnover.

The new rules in Germany and Australia have been heavily challenged on a number of intellectual grounds, including that they impinge on freedom of speech. But they are also hard to impose – history shows us that when one seemingly undesirable Internet-enabled app is knocked down, another similar one emerges. It's like playing whack-a-mole.

I argue that we should support governments in their efforts to regulate tech companies in the interests of reducing social harms. We should also campaign for tech companies to take self-regulation more seriously and ensure any new digital innovations are ethically sound. But we have to be realistic. The Internet is simply too vast, too complex and crosses too many borders for any one government or company to properly regulate it. Governments, just like parents, find it hard to manage the Internet through rule-based strategies alone.

For now, we need to look elsewhere. We need to see what we can do to take back control.

Taking back control

It is easy to blame governments and the makers of technology as they struggle to police the Internet. But how often to do we really turn the lens onto ourselves? I often forget, as I get distracted by my smartphone, that I bought the technology. I choose what apps to download, I decide how and when I use them – I am, ultimately, in control. When I recognise this, I start on the path to wisdom. I understand that I have the power to make rational and critical decisions. I understand that I must trust my better judgements.

This is good news. This means I don't have to wait for Big Tech or governments to get started on making my cyber-world a place I want to live in. Governments and Big Tech companies still have a great deal of responsibility to do their bit – this book is not about letting them off. I just don't have to wait for them to get their acts together.

I am not making a call for less use of cyber-technology; I am making a call for wiser use of cyber-technology.

It is a call for us to ensure that technology, like the Internet, is used to further the common good, or, at the least, not to undermine it. This means not waiting for others to regulate on our behalf, but for us to self-regulate. Self-regulation requires us to harness the power and possibilities of our characters and to champion the power and possibilities of our children's characters. This is how we will take back control from technology.

I am writing this book as a remedy for my own difficult relationship with cyber-technologies. I am writing it for my children. I am writing it because I believe in human nature and the power of character. I am writing it to show how through dedicated parenting and teaching we can help our children to flourish in the cyber-world. To flourish is to possess qualities that allow us to grow mentally, physically, socially and emotionally. To flourish is to possess the character virtues and practical wisdom that allow us to shape our cyber-worlds for the better.

Since the days of Aristotle, people have been thinking and writing about the importance of character for human flourishing. This book draws on these age-old theories and shows how they are perhaps more important than ever. More surprisingly, they are also just as applicable.

Activity: Rules, consequences or character – where do you stand?

Respond to the statements below concerning your attitudes to rules, consequences and character in the cyber-world.

Rules

Question	Agree	Somewhat agree	Not sure	Somewhat disagree	Disagree
I don't pay much attention to the terms and conditions of the Internet apps I download.					
I know children who bypass the age restrictions on social media websites.					
I believe that my children can get around some restrictions I place on Internet use and content.					
I think that most big Internet technology companies can't be regulated by governments.					
It is easy to watch paid-for TV like sport on the Internet for free.					
I don't believe the Big Tech companies are that interested in regulating themselves.					
I don't know the copyright rules for pictures I find on Google.					

Consequences

Question	Agree	Somewhat agree	Not sure	Somewhat disagree	Disagree
I might have hurt someone accidently through my online communication.					
I don't know how my children's use of their smartphones will affect their mental and physical health in the future.					
I don't know what all my online friends think of my social media posts.					
I don't know where everything I write online ends up.					
There are things I have written and posted online in the past that I worry will come back to haunt me.					

Character

Question	Agree	Somewhat agree	Not sure	Somewhat disagree	Disagree
If people were kinder to each other online, the cyber-world would be a better place.					
I worry about fake news online and wish I could trust everything I read on the Internet.					
I am ultimately in control of what I say or do online.					
My children are ultimately in control of what they say or do online.					

If you answered mostly agree or somewhat agree to these questions in all the sections, then you believe that character is important. You also recognise the limitations of consequence- and rules-based strategies for ensuring cyber-flourishing in the digital age.

If you answered somewhat disagree or disagree to most of the questions, you are more confident that rules- and consequence-based strategies, designed to enhance cyber-flourishing, can work.

CHAPTER 1: KEY MESSAGES

- We must try not to be technologically deterministic and to understand instead that bad things don't have to happen just because the Internet exists.

- This means we must focus on making *better* humans, not just on making *better* technologies. It's not about less technology but about wiser use of technology.

- We should call on governments and tech companies to (self-) regulate in the interests of making the cyber-world a better place to live, but we can't rely on them to do so. Our character and our wisdom therefore really matter.

2
Parenting in the Cyber-age

The cyber-age

'Vague but exciting' is how Sir Tim Berners-Lee's proposal for what was to become the World Wide Web was described by his boss in 1989. Today, more than half the world is online and connected to everyone else online though this web. The technology has spread more rapidly than any other in history. Perhaps unsurprisingly for such a new thing, the language we use to describe the Internet has not kept up with the pace at which the technology has developed. This language is inconsistent and changeable, creating something of a semantic minefield for those who write about it. Books, papers and media articles use different terms largely interchangeably. The Internet is variously known as 'cyberspace', 'the net', 'the web' and other such terms. Names have come and gone; for example, not that long ago the *information superhighway* was a popular term.

This is not a book for those looking for a deep investigation into definitions and concepts. However, I do need to say something about the terms I use in the book, as they will both help clarify what I am talking about and make my core argument. I will primarily use the term *cyber* in this book to describe the Internet and its associated technologies, and software.

Cyber: To successfully navigate the Internet's moral terrain

It was in the 1990s that the use of the term 'cyber'[1] came back into fashion. It was primarily used as a prefix; think how popular words like cyberspace are today. The term 'cyber' also has an older history, which is of particular importance for the argument I am making. It is this older history that is the reason I have chosen to use the term 'cyber', rather than, say, 'digital'. The choice of the term 'cyber' might seem odd given that it is often associated with negative connotations such as cyber-war and cyber-bullying. I want to reclaim the word. I want to do this by going back to its etymology.

Two thousand years ago, the term *kybernetes* meant 'helmsman' in Greek. This translation fits neatly with the core argument made in this book. The Internet exists and is unlikely to go away in the near future. What matters is how our children, indeed all of us, steer our way through it. We need to see ourselves as the helmsmen of the Internet – in charge of how we use it and in charge of its direction. The mouse, trackpad, keypad and touchscreen might be considered tillers, which we must use to steer through calm and stormy waters. What should we use to navigate with? We need a compass, or to be more precise, a moral compass. Those with a moral compass possess character; they know what the right course of action is in any given situation. They know the *right* way to go.

Debates on whether our children are born moral or not are far-reaching. One thing we can be sure of is that they are not born knowing how to use their moral compass to steer their way through their cyber-worlds. Our role is not to steer the ship for them, but to teach them how to use their compass more wisely. Perhaps in making this assertion I am assuming too much. Do we, as adults, know how to successfully navigate the ethical contours of the Internet?

This is an important point, as navigating the Internet is not easy because the multiple paths it offers are not familiar. This means we have to start by educating ourselves. We need to think about how we steer our way through our cyber-worlds and what we are modelling for our children. This is a point that I will come back to throughout the book – that our children's cyber-wisdom starts with our own cyber-wisdom, which is predicated on us having at least a basic cyber-literacy. We know what we are talking about and can share knowledge with our children because we share a common language.

The point, for now, is that the etymology of the word *cyber* helps us to think in terms of navigation and about how we have the freedom to choose how we travel in the cyber-world. The implication is that our combined educational efforts need to be directed at becoming better helmsmen by cultivating cyber-wisdom. The advice contained in this book will help all of us steer through the familiar as well as the less familiar, choppy and sometimes disorienting waters of the cyber-world.

How I use the term cyber in this book

'Cyber' is a word that reminds us we are in charge of how we use Internet-enabled technology. 'Cyber' can therefore be used as a useful prefix for four concepts that are central to the main arguments of this book, and I use them throughout. They are:

Cyber-world

For the purposes of this book, the cyber-world might be thought of as a world within a world. If we can separate the online world from the 'real' world, we can look closely at how the invention of the Internet has made particular demands on our children's character.

I acknowledge that this separation is not absolute, as the cyber-world and real world are one and the same. We should not be allowing our children to think that it is acceptable to behave differently in each world and that immoral behaviour is more permissible online than it is elsewhere. It is dangerous to think that what happens in the cyber-world has no crossover into the real world. It does in at least two ways. First, what happens online often spills over to the 'real' world. Think of an argument on social media that carries on in the classroom. Second, our children develop qualities in the 'real' world that they should show in the cyber-world and, importantly, vice versa. Playing games online, interacting on social media and other online activities can build character in the same way as volunteering and playing sport.

So, when I use the term cyber-world, my intention is not to divorce it from the 'real' world. The cyber-world exists within the wider world.

Cyber-wisdom

As you will probably understand by now, character and character education are at the heart of this book. What is the most important quality of character? For me, it is wisdom.

Wisdom is the decisions and judgements we make about how to apply our character in specific situations and contexts – what might also be called digital good sense. Cyber-wisdom is good sense enacted in the cyber-world. True cyber-wisdom is the expression of autonomous decision making and virtuous action. It is, as I will explain throughout this book, about making the right decision at the right time.

Cyber-wisdom can be learnt but it can't be taught – at least not through instruction. We cannot *make* our children be cyber-wise. We can show them exemplars of cyber-wisdom and we can point out when we think they have demonstrated cyber-wisdom (or not), but we cannot force them to possess this quality just by telling them to.

Cyber-wisdom is developed over a lifetime. It is developed through experience. No one can ever be fully cyber-wise, as the invention of new technologies will demand that we all learn how to use them with critical discernment and in a way that contributes to our own and others' flourishing. No one is born cyber-wise; it is honed over time and with conscious and continuous hard work.

Cyber-virtues

Apart from cyber-wisdom, which might be best considered a meta-virtue, there are other virtues that are particularly important for children to develop if they are to flourish online. A quick note here about the term *virtue*. I use it because the ancient moral theory of virtue ethics is at the foundation of this book. It is, I acknowledge, a term that has somewhat gone out of fashion. Virtues, for me, are modern-day human qualities that all of us must develop if we are to get on with each other. If you don't like the term virtue please substitute it with something like human quality, strength, disposition or trait.

My research shows honesty and compassion are the most pertinent virtues for children living with digital technologies, as they relate to their most pressing online moral concerns. There are growing concerns about whether we can trust the content we access online –

so-called fake news. Also, concerns about the rise of online plagiarism and piracy are chiefly about honesty. The virtue of compassion is linked to some of the most persistent moral concerns for most parents, teachers and children today, such as cyber-bullying, trolling and sexting. Other cyber-virtues are also important for successful online living and these include courage, humility, gratitude, integrity, service, justice, resilience and many others. Cyber-virtues are explored in more detail when I explain the components of the REACT and THRIVE models. For now, you just need to know that the cultivation and honing of cyber-virtues is one of the key areas that I believe education must focus on.

Cyber-flourishing

Cyber-flourishing should be the goal that we aim towards, for ourselves, our children and, more broadly, the society we live in. It is the aim to live well in a cyber-world worth living in.

Flourishing is not about hedonistic pleasure or simply having fun. It is something more authentic, deep and sustaining. It is the sense of wellbeing, harmony and genuine happiness we experience when we feel that we are contributing positively to our (cyber-) world.

The more people who possess cyber-wisdom and cyber-virtues, the more likely that global cyber-flourishing will become a reality.

What cyber-technologies am I talking about in this book?

The terminology we use to describe the Internet and its associated technologies is changeable and not very specific. For this reason, I want to be clear *what* technologies I am talking about in this book.

It is useful to think in terms of cyber-hardware and cyber-software. Most cyber-hardware technologies, such as tablets, smartphones, laptops and televisions, are digital. Digital, in its most literal form, means how 1s and 0s are used by technology to communicate with other technology and aid how we communicate. Although the Internet has many uses, it is this form of digital communication that has probably been the most revolutionary, and it plays a large role in this book.

While a tablet might be used by a toddler to watch television, this is not my primary concern. Watching television, at least for now, might be considered a largely passive and unidirectional activity. When the same tablet is used for communication with others, it becomes a tool for interaction. It is when we interact with others that we are most often called upon to show our true character and make wise decisions. It requires us to engage, think and react well. My aim is to show how we can help our children interact more successfully when using connected cyber-hardware – devices such as smartphones, tablets, laptops and networked gaming systems.

If cyber-hardware is the gadget, the tools we can physically touch, cyber-software is what makes it all work. This book is actually not so much about the hardware our children use, but the way they use it.

We can't touch or hold software applications, but they are more powerful than the hardware itself. In its simplest form, software might be considered a whole bunch of code that tells the hardware what to do. Examples of cyber-software include email, social media, instant messaging, video messaging, games and many others. Some of the features of these digital communication technologies are:

- they afford users the opportunity for instant communication in written, visual or auditory forms;

- they can connect users to one or many people;

- they allow for synchronous or asynchronous communication;

- and, they are accessible at almost any time and any place.

It is the use of these interactive features, built into the software, that makes particular demands on character.

At what age does this matter?

An obvious question is whether I have written this book for parents (and teachers) with children of a particular age? The short answer is I have not, but the longer answer is more complicated than that. This is because when in your child's life the core messages in this book become relevant depends on a number of factors, including when your children first enter the cyber-world, their developmental stage, and their individual personality and character qualities.

Many children will first encounter cyber-technologies at a very young age. Many of us have given our child a phone or tablet as a form of babysitter, to keep them busy when we are busy. I have done the same, and in this book I don't make a judgement on when it is appropriate to let your child have their own cyber-technology. This book is about when children start using the interactive features of cyber-technologies, such as those central to social media.

Clearly, there is a concern that this might start happening for some children earlier than we think. The UK's National Crime Agency, based on its investigators' experiences of how sex offenders try to groom children online, have started to make educational programmes for children as young as four years old. Although their materials, including film clips and stories, do not refer to child sexual abuse, they do teach children to recognise techniques used by paedophiles. For some parents the lessons contained in this book will be relevant even before their children have started school.

For me, things got real when my daughter got her first phone at the age of eleven. My daughter was not the first nor the last in her peer group to get a smartphone. A recent survey by Childwise found that it is normal for children to get their first phone when they are seven years old.[2] Like the parents of my daughter's friends, you must choose when it is the right time for your children. You should choose a time when you think they are ready to take on the responsibility. After all, although we buy the technology and we provide the scaffolding when they first start using it, it is our children who have to be the builders.

Activity: Cyber-wisdom taught and caught

A good way to think about character development is to think about how character qualities are caught, and taught.[3] Complete the table below to think about what you currently do, or might do in the future, to be more intentional in your approach to educating cyber-virtues for cyber-flourishing.

Taught: What do you do explicitly to help your children develop knowledge, understanding and skills that contribute to their development of cyber-wisdom and cyber-virtues?	Caught: What you do, implicitly or explicitly, to create an ethos and environment that make it more likely your children will develop cyber-virtues and cyber-wisdom?
Example: I speak to my children about the importance of being kind online.	Example: I try to exemplify the types of qualities that I hope my children will show online.
I explain . . .	I think my children notice when I . . .
I found an activity online that helped my children learn about . . .	I share examples of . . .

CHAPTER 2: KEY MESSAGES

• The etymology of the word *cyber* is helmsman. We must help our children develop character qualities that help them to successfully navigate their cyber-worlds.

• The necessity to cultivate these qualities kicks in as soon as our children start using the interactive features of the technology.

• The ultimate goal is to cultivate cyber-wisdom in children so they can live well in a cyber-world worth living in.

3
From Online Risks to Online Opportunities

Are the kids really all right?

In 1997, soon after the Internet really took off, Jon Katz wrote a book entitled *Virtuous Reality*.[1] Katz's central argument was that the 'kids are all right' and children will thrive in the digital world as long as adults leave them to it. Katz's firmly held belief was that not only were children the founders of the digital world, but they were also very capable of being good custodians of it. A similar line of argument has been pursued by others since. In his seminal work *Growing up Digital*[2] Don Tapscott predicted a moral panic about the Internet and digital technologies. He wrote, 'concerns about the Internet, by cynics, moralists or technophobes, are plain wrong'. Tapscott's contention was that children are flourishing in the digital world and that we should leave them to it, as, after all, they know more about how it works than adults. A recent book by Jordan Shapiro[3] argues that we must rethink our attitudes to technology. He believes that fear and nostalgia are powerful enemies and stand in the way of our children's best interests. Shapiro makes his case on progressive grounds, that it is us, adults, who must change our attitudes.

The thrust of the argument that Katz and Tapscott made twenty years ago and Shapiro makes today is that we should trust children to navigate their cyber-worlds. However, these books are in the minority. For every book or newspaper article that argues the Internet is a force for good, there are many that detail its negative effects on childhood. It is not the purpose of this book to weigh up this argument, and in any case, it would take several books to do so. However, I must say something about the possibly negative effects of the Internet on children and young people, otherwise there would be no need for you to read this book. If Katz, Tapscott and Shapiro are right and the 'kids are all right' then we can pretty much leave our children to it.

I don't believe this is the case. I think the Internet does present concerns, some of which can have serious consequences not just for our children but also for the wider world. This is why we have a responsibility to be interventionists. We should not seek to turn back time, restrict access or use, but we must be intentional in educating our children to help them to thrive in their cyber-worlds.

Moral perception, not moral panic

Fears about the influence of the Internet on children reflect previous moral panics about new technologies. Negative reaction greeted the advent of film in the early twentieth century, radio in the 1920s and television in the 1940s. Concerns about the Internet could follow a similar pattern to these so-called moral panics. Each started with concerns about access to, and the time young people spent with, the new technologies (often called screen-time). They then moved to the content children are exposed to through the technology and the possible negative effect it will have on them.

In 2016 a poll of 1,738 parents of eleven- to seventeen-year-olds from across the UK found that parents' attitudes towards social media were largely negative – more than half of parents believed that social media hinders or undermines a young person's character and moral development. Only 15 per cent of respondents agreed that social media could 'enhance or support' it.[4]

This finding might be explained by the almost daily news stories about one or more of the following concerns:

Cyber-bullying
Internet piracy
Pornography
Harmful and offensive content
Online stalking

Paedophilia
Stealth marketing
Abuse of personal information
Online gambling addition
Abuse of privacy
Digital legacies
Fake news
Hacking
... and many others.

Most of these issues are not unique to the Internet, but rather are manifestations of offline problems – digital technologies might simply have modernised moral concerns, and in some cases, amplified them. For example:

- Piracy today is of much greater concern due to the ease with which music and other content can be downloaded for free.

- Stalking and paedophilia are of greater concern due to fears over anonymity and the new possibilities for connections being forged between strangers.

- Pornography is a greater concern due to the lack of restrictions and gatekeepers online – it is more freely and widely available than ever.

- Bullying is a greater concern as it can now take place at any time and in any place.

Although the academic literature tends to be more balanced in its viewpoint, it is possible to find writers predicting dangerous outcomes for children and young people. Some commentators have even suggested that digital technologies might end up being responsible for the destruction of childhood.

These are pejorative views and dismissed by many as being reactionary and over the top. More sober arguments about negative effects have, however, been made by reputable sources. For example, consider these reports from the last few years:

2017: A report by The Royal Society for Public Health stated that 'social media may be fuelling a mental health crisis' in young people. Instagram is rated as the worst social media platform when it comes to its impact on young people's mental health.[5]

2017: The Millennium Cohort Study based on fourteen-year-olds' reporting of their emotional problems found that 24 per cent of girls and 9 per cent of boys suffer from depression. Links to the Internet are made throughout the report.[6]

2019: The United Kingdom Chief Medical Officer recommends a precautionary approach to managing how much exposure to screen-time our children have. A systematic map of reviews showed a potential link between screen-time and mental health issues, including anxiety and depression.[7]

2019: The House of Commons Science and Technology committee research into the impact of social media and screen-use on young people's health discusses the benefits (friendship and support, creativity and learning, health advice) and the risks of social media and screens. The risks include: physical health and low activity, harm from electromagnetic fields, overuse of screen-time, poor mental health and wellbeing, pornography, hate speech, violence, fake news, grooming, sexting, cyber-bullying and negative body image. The report does, however, point out that the research evidence is unclear if the risks actually lead to harm.[8]

Let's now look at reports that focus on a single issue: cyber-bullying.

Reports from academics, government bodies and charities in recent years have found that:

- Those who experience cyber-bullying are 2.3 times more likely to self-harm, 2.1 times more likely to exhibit suicidal behaviour and 2.5 times more likely to attempt suicide than those who don't.[9]

- In the USA, 43 per cent of teens reported being victims of cyber-bullying in 2007; 18 per cent of males and 16 per cent of females admitted that they bully others online; 75 per cent of teens know who is cyber-bullying them. Nearly 30 per cent of teens desire to seek revenge on those who have cyber-bullied them.[10]

- A report from Childline showed that between 2012 and 2013, cyber-bullying concerns were mentioned by young people in 4,507 counselling sessions, an increase of 87 per cent when compared to 2011/12. This is a sharp rise, considering there was a 4 per cent decline in overall bullying counselling.[11]

- A Public Health England report showed that cyber-bullying is associated with socio-economic status. Young people from more affluent families were more likely to report being victims of cyber-bullying. The report also showed that in the UK 17.9 per cent of eleven- to fifteen-year-olds reported being cyber-bullied in the two months prior to being surveyed, that girls were twice as likely as boys to report being cyber-bullied, and that the reported prevalence rates of cyber-bullying at age fifteen were almost double those for eleven-year-olds.[12]

These reports make for alarming reading for any parent of a child entering the cyber-world. No parent wants their child to be bullied or to be a bully themselves.

Other concerns that have been prompted by the Internet include the shallowing thesis proposed by Nicolas Carr.[13] His argument is that cyber-technologies are making us unable to concentrate and focus on one thing. This is an argument that has also been made popular by Cal Newport, Professor of Computer Science at Georgetown University, in his book *Deep Work*. A regular commentator in the news these days is neuroscientist Susan Greenfield, who has repeatedly claimed that overuse of computers is rewiring our children's brains and could be causing behavioural issues, attention deficit disorder and even autism.[14] It is perhaps for these reasons that one of the more popular schools in Silicon Valley is a Waldorf Steiner school where screens are largely banned. If the people who are inventing and peddling the technology are not allowing their children to use it – at least at school – then what is it they know that we don't?

But there is another side to this picture. One that is more positive.

If you look for them, it is not hard to find stories in newspapers that highlight the power of cyber-technology as a force for good. Think about Martha Payne from Scotland who, at twelve years old, got more than three million hits on her blog about improving school meals. Or, the #iwill campaign that has highlighted the stories of children who have used technology to make a meaningful difference to others through social action. For example, young people who take photos of places that need cleaning up, and then post them on Facebook as a call to action. Groups of young people then come together to clean up the area and post new pictures showing the difference they have made. Recently, there have been stories in the newspapers about how young people are using TikTok to post fifteen-second videos about issues that matter to them such as gun crime and climate change. These videos are downloaded in their millions.

These examples highlight the potential for the Internet to be a force for good, a tool that brings us together, that can unite us and help us work in aid of worthy causes. Michael Sanders and Susannah Hume have made a similar point in their book *Social Butterflies: Reclaiming the Positive Power of Social Networks*. Introducing the book, the authors write about social media:

Even when things seem quite dark, it's important to remember that the majority of acts, by the majority of people, are positive. By understanding the beauty of our social selves, and by supporting people to build better, more supportive networks, we can find new ways to work towards a kinder, fairer world.[15]

For these authors, technology plus good character should be the basis for transforming society for the better.

Online risks, online opportunities

Given this unclear picture, it is perhaps not surprising that many discussions in the academic literature go to great lengths to present balanced arguments about the positive and negative influence of the Internet on us. Consider this comment by David Clough. Although the quote is over fifteen years old, I believe it stands the test of time.

On the one hand, there are the exuberant enthusiasts who see 'cyberspace' as a new frontier promising freedom, democracy, knowledge, adventure and requiring the reinvention of all human social and political structures. On the other there are those who fear the Internet is giving unrestricted opportunities for pornographers, paedophiles, and drug traffickers, and leading to a future in which all human interaction is reduced to bits and bytes.[16]

For me, this quotation summarises, in just two sentences, the core arguments of thousands of articles I have read about the angst, uncertainty, hopes and fears we have about the Internet.

No one in the UK has done more to outline the risks and opportunities the Internet affords our children than Sonia Livingstone.[17] In 2009, Sonia conducted an analysis of studies in an attempt to understand the potential effects of the Internet on children. The analysis was no easy task, as the literature ranges across the disciplines of education, psychology, information science and health, as well as new emergent sub-disciplines, such as cyber-ethics. Livingstone acknowledges that there is potential for the risks and opportunities to overlap, and her analysis provides an excellent summary of the literature in the field.

Sonia Livingstone's Online Opportunities and Risks[18]

Online Risks	Online Opportunities
Illegal content	Access to global information
Paedophiles, grooming, strangers	Educational resources
Extreme or sexual violence	Social networking among friends
Harmful, offensive content	Entertainment, games, fun
Racist / hate material / activities	User-generated content-creation
Advertising and stealth marketing	Civic or political participation
Biased or misinformation	Privacy for identity expression
Abuse of personal information	Community involvement / activism
Cyber-bullying, harassment	Technological expertise / literacy
Gambling / phishing / financial scams	Career advancement / employability
Self-harm (suicide, anorexia)	Personal / health / sexual advice
Invasions / abuse of privacy	Specialist groups / fan forums
Illegal activities (hacking, copyright abuse)	Shared experiences with distant others

We cannot tell at this stage if the Internet is, on balance, a force for good or bad. This is why I like Livingstone's table of risks and opportunities. It shows us the best and the worst of the Internet. The analysis has not been carried out to further a moral panic but to give us some perception – to paint a picture of how the Internet might affect the moral lives of children.

Maximising the opportunities and minimising the risks

The argument I make in this book is that we need education that focuses on character and cyber-wisdom to ensure our children spend more of their time doing the things on the left of Livingstone's table and less time experiencing the things on the right. This education should enable them to maximise the opportunities and minimise the risks.

Crucially, not knowing what is really going on is not a reason for inaction. It is, in fact, more of a reason to act. The cyber-worlds our children live in are dynamic and changing. Our children are complex; their emotional and social needs are also constantly changing. No single intervention will solve every concern. However, a clearly defined educational approach based on sound theory could. This theory must take into account common understandings of how children develop, and it must also accommodate the changing nature of childhoods. I have argued that this theory should be informed by the moral philosophy called virtue ethics.

Virtue ethics prioritises character as the basis for making wise moral decisions; decisions that minimise online risks and maximise online opportunities. In the next chapter I will explain why I believe this to be the case.

Activity: Hopes and fears

On a blank piece of paper write down the hopes and fears that you have for the Internet. Make a list for yourself and one for your children. It might also be interesting to make a list of the hopes and fears you have about the impact of the Internet on society more generally.

Once you have made the two or three lists, think about what it would take for you and your children to be able to realise more of the hopes (opportunities) and experience fewer of your fears (risks) that you have identified. For some of the actions you identify, you will likely need to involve other people, institutions and organisations – think about who these are and what, if any, influence you have over them. Hopefully you will see that for many of the items on your list, you and your children have full or some control over them. The difference between your hopes and your fears will likely be such character qualities as courage, compassion, honesty, gratitude, humility, resilience, civility, love and integrity.

As a follow-up, you might want to do the activity again with your children. You can then compare your lists and theirs, and this could be a great way to start a conversation about your shared hopes and fears.

CHAPTER 3: KEY MESSAGES

- We should be positive about the potential of the Internet to contribute to both individual and societal flourishing – but we must also be realistic.

- We must have moral perception – not contribute to moral panics. This means learning about and understanding the ethical challenges that have come with the invention of the Internet.

- We should also recognise that the picture is more complex and celebrate the ways the Internet can be used as a force for good in local, national and international communities.

- The difference between our children being exposed to online risks and seizing online opportunities often depends on their character and their cyber-wisdom.

4

From Digital Natives to Cyber-citizens

Digital natives

Our children might be described as born digital, but does this make them digital natives?

It was Marc Prensky, the American educator, who was credited as the first person to use the term 'digital natives'.[1] Using dramatic language, he describes the change that has befallen our children:

> A really big discontinuity has taken place. One might even call it a 'singularity' – an event which changes things so fundamentally that there is absolutely no going back. This so-called 'singularity' is the arrival and rapid dissemination of digital technology in the last decades of the twentieth century.

Prensky contrasts digital natives – those who were born in a digital era and learnt organically to use technology – against digital immigrants – those who had to adapt to the digital era and formally learn how to use technology. Prensky's argument has some merit if we look at the fact that:

- children today watch more television online (predominantly via YouTube) than on television sets;

- children today can be active creators rather than simple passive consumers of the media;

- children today have arguably a much greater voice and efficacy than their parents did at their age;

- children today can communicate with friends and others 24/7;

- children today do not play games with those in the same space, but with friends and strangers around the world.

All of these things might also be true of adults, but Prensky's point is that we have had to adapt to these changes. Prensky is making a two-tribes argument. Many others have followed suit. The seemingly innate connection between children and the Internet can be charted by the one-upmanship among commentators to find terms to label the phenomenon. Here are a few: 'app generation'; 'cyberkids'; 'digital natives'; 'N generation'; 'n-geners'; and 'Google generation'. The statistics would seem to back up the use of these labels. Most point to the almost ubiquitous use of mobile phones, the Internet and other digital technologies by children over the age of eleven.

What is interesting about these statistics is how global they appear to be. Rates of Internet use are similar in most developed countries around the world. At this juncture, it is important to note that although almost half the world uses the Internet, half the world is not online. This is a useful reminder that we should be wary of making any universal claims about Internet use and its effects. We must read beyond the statistics to gain a truer picture about what is really going on. We have to watch and study our own children over time if we want to know how the Internet is affecting them.

Digital natives or cyber-citizens?

I think the term digital native is a neat and practical way to describe the difference between how our children experience childhood and how their parents experienced it. However, when we dig deeper, I don't think it is that useful as a concept to help us understand what is really going on online.

To be a native is to presuppose a person is born in and identifies with a specified place. Natives can say where they are native to, even if they don't like the place. It might be true that young people born anytime in the last two decades have been born in a digital world, but this does not mean they identify or even live in this world. Research shows there is a form of digital poverty in the UK and other countries, and that some children cannot afford laptops, smartphones and other gadgets, meaning they are unable to fully embrace the Internet. In contrast, some consider access to the Internet a human right these days.

We should be critical of any account that claims that all children are constant consumers of technology, that they are permanently online, able to rapidly assimilate multimedia information and to consume data simultaneously from different sources. To be considered a 'native' is a loaded term, as it assumes a person associates with a particular culture while understanding its unwritten rules. I think it is more helpful to think of children and young people who *choose* to interact with the digital world as cyber-citizens. It invites us to make a value judgement: what sort of cyber-citizen are they?

Cyber-citizens: Technology plus character

To be called digital natives suggests our children innately know how to use digital technologies because they have grown up with them. To be called a cyber-citizen demands something more. To be called a cyber-citizen our children must:

> know how to use the technology;

AND

> know how to use it as a force for good.

A cyber-citizen is therefore someone who uses cyber-technologies to enhance human flourishing. This requires that younger users of the Internet have not simply technical knowledge or proficiency, but also character. It is only when technical knowledge and character are combined that the Internet can become a force for good. Social networks that change the world for the better occur when technological know-how meets *good* character.

Just as we cannot expect technological proficiency to grow innately in our children, we also cannot expect that our children will simply acquire virtues and cyber-wisdom. We put increasing amounts of time into teaching our children how to code and use digital technologies in order to become what is often called digitally literate. This is a digital proficiency in a fairly instrumental sense.

We need to put equal or more time into educating our children to possess character as we do into educating them to possess knowledge and skills. Some of the best-known people of the last century have said the same. Martin Luther King Jr said, in his famous 'I Have a Dream' speech, that 'knowledge and character is the true goal of education', and one of Mahatma Gandhi's seven social sins was 'knowledge without character'. Their argument was that to possess (technological) knowledge without character can be dangerous and harmful. The following letter by a survivor of a Nazi concentration camp makes this point more poignantly than I can:

Dear Teacher:

I am a survivor of a concentration camp. My eyes saw what no man should witness:

Gas chambers built by learned engineers.

Children poisoned by educated physicians.

Infants killed by trained nurses.

Women and babies shot and burned by high school and college graduates.

So, I am suspicious of education.

My request is: Help your students become human. Your efforts must never produce learned monsters, skilled psychopaths, educated Eichmanns.

Reading, writing, arithmetic are important only if they serve to make our children more human.[2]

We might update this last line to *learning computing is important only if it serves to make our children more human.*

This means that learning must focus on the cultivation of ethical skills and minds. Of course, for true transformation to take place, this learning must occur on a grand scale. Education must aim at gaining a critical mass of those living in the cyber-world to possess character *and* technological proficiency. Aristotle made a distinction between different types of knowledge; one he called *techne* (technical know-how) and the other *phronesis* (moral know-how).[3] We need our children to possess both types of knowledge and to ensure that they work in harmony.

This means we must think beyond our children simply being digital natives and possessing digital literacy. We must ask what we are doing to help them become cyber-citizens – cyber-citizens with good character who possess cyber-wisdom. We must think about what role we have in making this dream a possibility.

Our responsibility as digital immigrants

I have made a case that it is not enough for our children to be content with being digital natives who are cyber-competent in a purely practical sense. They must also seek to be cyber-citizens with cyber-wisdom. We can't assume children will simply develop into good cyber-citizens by chance or good luck. We have to be intentional in our approach to education for cyber-citizenship. We must act with purpose and conviction. This means we have to think about it, plan it, reflect on it and, of course, take action when required. This is a considerable responsibility for those of us who might, in Prensky's language, consider ourselves to be digital immigrants.

While I have taken some issue with the term digital natives, I find the idea of digital immigrants more useful. The language of migration helps us adults who are not born digital to think about the cyber-world we are increasingly living in, whether by choice or not. Like most immigrants, we have to learn new rules and a new language and adapt to new cultural and social norms.

Migrants are often thought of in two ways: as those who make a move into another place voluntarily and those who are forced to move. I believe that we must strive to be in the former category if we are to help our children flourish in their cyber-worlds. Voluntary migration is undertaken by people who have freedom to choose. They are going into the new place with their eyes wide open, having undertaken research and decided that they like much of what they see. Forced migration is undertaken by people who, through events outside their control, have been made to move, sometimes against their will. We have to move voluntarily into the cyber-world our children live in and we have to want to live in this world with them. It is ultimately up to us if we want to settle there, but at the very least we need to explore the place and try to learn about it.

Successful settlers, explorers and migrants need to learn new languages, adopt different attitudes, change their ways of doing things, reach out to people who they don't know, participate, be interactive, be open, be courageous, be tolerant, try to understand and act with compassion and care. Settlers and explorers also bring their experience, expertise and wisdom with them, but they have to apply these to different sets of situations and contexts. They have to be adaptable and creative.

Our differing experiences and knowledge mean that we can't easily show our children how to live online. We can't do this for them; we have to learn with them. We have to be partners in learning how to live in the cyber-world, each of us bringing our differing experiences, qualities and knowledge.

How should we become voluntary immigrants?

We become good voluntary digital immigrants through a process of active assimilation. Passive assimilation is to adopt a negative attitude to new technologies and hope they will go away, or to complain about them endlessly while being constantly on our smartphones. Active assimilation is being open to and excited about the possibilities that technologies bring us, while still being aware of their pitfalls. It is to purposely venture out and try to learn about new technologies, to understand them better. It is to seek out opportunities to learn about the technologies from people and, perhaps most importantly, from our own children.

Someone who has taken steps to actively assimilate is more likely to seek reasons to accept rather than reject their new world. They are more likely to feel excited by its possibilities and less likely to fear it. They are in a better position to control it freely, rather than let it control them. We must be voluntary digital immigrants if we are truly to help our children thrive online. We must accept the challenge ahead of us and be excited by it. We must recognise that we have an experience and wisdom that we can bring to this world, but we must adapt these qualities to suit the new contexts we find ourselves in.

This requires us not to be character teachers, but to act as character coaches.

Coaches and teachers are both types of educators, but they operate in different ways. A classic image of a teacher would be someone leading from the front, imparting knowledge based on their expertise. Coaches, on the other hand, are no less participatory but they are responding as well as leading. They are always looking to help shape or form someone, but doing so through responding to what they see, not just what they know. Whereas a teacher might strive to pull children and young people towards a marked goal from the front, a coach would strive to push them towards this goal from a less dominant position.

If we are to act as a character coach, we must try to see communication more as a form of conversation than instruction, to see our children as individuals and their circumstances as unique and particular. We must seek to respond, as much as lead and act spontaneously, rather than sticking to a script.

It is of course helpful to have some guidance about how we can best undertake this role. A rigid script is not desirable, but some pointers about what sort of approach we should take are. I provide this in the form of the REACT and THRIVE models (see Part Two and Part Three).

Helping the Internet to grow up

I am optimistic about the possibility that cyber-technologies can transform the world for the better.

As I have explained, my core argument is that we control the technologies and therefore we, as a collective, can ensure that the Internet's amazing power can be used as a force for good. If we are in charge of navigating the ship, then we can decide where we want it to go. Though it might feel for some as though we have let the ship sail away and it is too late, this is not my contention. It is also not the contention of Sir Tim Berners-Lee, the inventor of the World Wide Web. On its thirtieth anniversary in 2019, Sir Tim said in an open letter:

> Given how much the web has changed in the past 30 years, it would be defeatist and unimaginative to assume that the web as we know it can't be changed for the better in the next 30. If we give up on building a better web now, then the web will not have failed us. We will have failed the web.[4]

Sir Tim then went on to say: 'The web is for everyone and collectively we hold the power to change it. It won't be easy. But if we dream a little and work a lot, we can get the web we want.'

I agree. It is too early to give up on the Internet. We could see its first thirty years as an experiment in which we learn how to be good custodians of the technology. This takes education.

It requires us to educate our children with character and cyber-wisdom to make Sir Tim's vision a reality.

I have never been educated about how I should behave online. My children and my friends' children receive some education on this, but it tends to come in the form of stand-alone sessions. This is not the type of education that is needed at this critical time in their lives. We need sustained, ingrained, deep educational experiences that really help children to steer or navigate their way successfully through their cyber-worlds. I believe that if we as parents and teachers adjust our educational approach by making it more explicit, reflective and focused on character and wisdom, then cyber-technologies can be redirected to ensure they are more universally used as a force for good.

The same features of the technologies that allow for cyber-bullying might also be used for cyber-citizenship projects on a mass scale that truly can change the world. To tackle global concerns including climate change, poverty and cyber- and other warfare, we need mass global cyber-citizenship projects that target these and other issues more than ever.

If we are to help the Internet grow up, we have to stop neglecting these important issues as we educate our children.

Activity: Is your child a digital native?

See how your children's use of the Internet compares to the average in the UK. The following statistics are from the 2018 Ofcom *Children and Parents: Media Use and Attitudes* report.[5]

Do your children own a smartphone?
83 per cent of twelve- to fifteen-year-olds own a smartphone.
35 per cent of eight- to eleven-year-olds own a smartphone.

Does your child own a tablet?
50 per cent of twelve- to fifteen-year-olds own a tablet.
47 per cent of eight- to eleven-year-olds own a tablet.

How long does your child play online games for each week?
76 per cent of twelve- to fifteen-year-olds play online games for over thirteen and a half hours a week.
74 per cent of eight- to eleven-year-olds play online games for over ten hours a week.

Is your child online for over twenty hours a week?
99 per cent of twelve- to fifteen-year-olds are online for at least twenty hours a week.

93 per cent of eight- to eleven-year-olds are online for at least thirteen and a half hours a week.

Does your child have a social media profile?

68 per cent of twelve- to fifteen-year-olds have a social media profile.

18 per cent of eight- to eleven-year-olds have a social media profile.

Is your child allowed to take their phone to bed with them?

71 per cent of twelve- to fifteen-year-olds who own a mobile phone are allowed to take it to bed with them.

40 per cent of eight- to eleven-year-olds who own a mobile phone are allowed to take it to bed with them.

CHAPTER 4: KEY MESSAGES

- It is not helpful to think of all children as digital natives – children use cyber-technologies in different ways, and some don't use them at all. We need to observe our children to see how they choose to use their technologies.

- We should be asking if our children are cyber-citizens. To be a cyber-citizen means they have chosen to use technologies in ways that contribute positively to the cyber- and non-cyber-world.

- To be a good cyber-citizen requires cyber-wisdom as well as technological know-how. It's about character and coding.

- We can help our children be better cyber-citizens if we choose to be voluntary digital immigrants – this means we must choose to engage in the cyber-worlds of our children.

5

Introducing the REACT and THRIVE Models

In this book, I introduce two models, REACT and THRIVE, that I have been honing, through research and practice, over the last decade. In this chapter, I explain why these models are needed to guide our parenting and teaching.

Why don't we just know what to do?

For most of my life I have believed that parenting is largely instinctive. I do not think my parents read a book to learn that I needed to be fed, clothed and given shelter. When I had children, I did not read a book to know that I had to provide these basic needs for my own children. Parenting at this functional level should be pretty instinctive.

What about when parenting goes beyond these basics? Did my parents have to read a book to learn about the values they wanted me to adopt? I don't think so. I try to teach my children what I think matters in life. What I think matters is informed by:

- what my immediate and wider family thinks is important;

- what those around me, with whom I share my life, think is important;

- a judgement on what I think wider society values.

For example, I encourage my children to behave well in public. Most parents I know do the same. This imperative has been passed down and through the ages.

This might be considered a form of *character caught*. My children have hopefully learnt, almost by osmosis, what is expected of them in different situations. I have not had any formal lessons about how to 'teach values'. I would think my friends very odd if they told me that they had had lessons on how to help their children to be kind or honest. These qualities, like many others, are developed in practice, over time, and reinforced through thousands of micro-interactions. I see this as part and parcel of the role of being a parent. I don't always get it right, but I hope I get it right enough times to ensure that most of what I value is passed on to my children.

So, why are there so many books on parenting out there? One reason is that they are a source of comfort when everything gets a bit too much. Soon after my daughter was born, sleep deprivation drove me to reading books on how to get babies to sleep. I actually remember thinking that it is not possible to be a parent after one particularly sleep-deprived night. I searched for a magic theory and practical strategies that would allow me and my wife to feel human again. It slowly dawned on me (probably at dawn) that there was no universal, sure-fire theory out there that would work. My daughter was unique. The advice in the books went from being helpful and reassuring to annoying. Helping my daughter to sleep and stay asleep was a challenge that my wife and I had to take on ourselves. We had to rely largely on our instinct.

In short, I have never felt I needed to turn to theory or an educational model to guide my parenting.

Until now.

I'll explain why.

New models for new challenges

The seismic changes that the Internet has made to our children's lives have happened so quickly. We have not had time to stop and think about what to do. Even if we had time, what would we use it for? We can't go back to learn from the past. We have been helping children to eat, sleep and play well with others for thousands of years. To guide us and learn how to undertake these roles successfully, we draw on the experiences, advice, wisdom and knowledge of those before us. In contrast, our parents and our grandparents never had to deal with the challenges that cyber-technologies have thrown at us. Networked gaming on a vast scale and instant and continuous communication through social networks bring new parenting challenges. We can't look at years of research to find answers about what to do. It's happening now, it is live and it is new.

You might rightly argue that concerns associated with the Internet, such as bullying, stalking and copyright violation, have been managed successfully in the past, so why can't we rely on old-fashioned solutions to deal with these issues today? I don't think this is possible. We can certainly seek to be informed by wisdom from the past, but we must ensure our parenting and teaching is relevant to the modern age. The affordances offered to all of us by technologies, such as the ability to be anonymous and communicate on a grand scale to widespread audiences, is different and new. Technology offers power and opportunities to children and young people born today that were not available to us. This brings new risks and opportunities, and we need new models and approaches to education to help us negotiate them.

If we can't look for advice from the past for help, then what can we learn from present-day research on how best to parent and teach in the digital age?

Can research help?

You might think there would be plenty of research that informs our parenting and teaching in the digital age. Unfortunately, there is not.

We need the REACT and THRIVE theory-based educational models because empirical research cannot yet tell us what we need to do. There are some helpful studies, but there is no research that supports a comprehensive and intentional approach to educating for cyber-wisdom. For now, we must draw on data when it is helpful and fill in the gaps with well-thought-out theory.

The REACT and THRIVE theoretical models provide a framework to guide educational practice. You will notice in the coming chapters that I provide evidence when it is available for the different approaches I outline. But first I'll explain the evidence gap in a bit more detail.

The following question may sound simple enough: 'How honest are children on social media profiles?' But to answer this question with any sense of accuracy is devilishly difficult.

I am an academic researcher who is trained to problematise, critique and question. These are the qualities you need to bring into play when reading articles that claim the Internet is affecting children or indeed any of us in particular ways. These articles often transfer to sensationalist newspaper headlines. Many of them are based on half-truths.

Amy Orben and her colleague Andrew Przybylski[1] undertook detailed research using large data sets to investigate the links between adolescence, wellbeing and digital technology use. They showed how easy it is, when running the data, to find headline-worthy results. However, their analysis also produced what is known as false positives; if the data was to be analysed again a different result would probably be found. Orben and Przybylski showed how they found many thousands of theoretically defensible analyses of negative correlation between technology use and wellbeing. However, they also showed they could run the data and find positive correlations between technology use and wellbeing.

We need to learn to think like scientists and to question the limitations and validity of different studies. Moral panics take hold when we don't. It would be disingenuous to the many thousands of excellent researchers working in this field around the world not to acknowledge that studies in the field are important and do help us know more. And if the Big Tech companies open up their massive data sets for the purposes of research directed at advancing cyber-flourishing, we will soon know more yet.

At the limits of what we know

I think it is important to understand why we can't rely on the data from many studies that examine the impact of technology on children. Why do we seemingly know so little given how much research is conducted in this area? There are six principal reasons:

1. **No two people are the same:** We often draw conclusions from large data sets, but not all individuals in them are the same. For example, one researcher might show that screen-time is bad for people. But there are different types of screen-time. One person's screen-time might be spent on occasional gaming, watching iPlayer, and using the Internet for homework. Another's screen-time might consist of spending hours looking at and posting selfies, watching porn or playing *Fortnite*. These people might spend the same amount of time in any one week online, but the effects of this screen-time on them are likely to be different. According to Dr Max Davie from the Royal College of Paediatrics and Child Health: 'The controversy around screen-use and adolescent wellbeing has always suffered from an excess of opinion relative to data.'[2] How do we ensure this nuance is included in studies? We need to get the message out that one size does not fit all.

2. **We can't keep up:** Think about how many different phones you have had in the last ten years and how many features and applications each of them contained. When the first phones came out, the novelty was in choosing a ringtone – I should know as I sold them for a short time in the late 1990s. The evolution of the smartphone has been staggering. The technology we keep in our pocket is more powerful than the most advanced super-computer invented several decades

ago. Different phones and different features are likely to have different effects on different people. Researchers struggle to keep up with the changes, particularly because to undertake good research takes time. This is why cross-sectional studies that provide findings valid at one point in time are limited. Much of this type of research is likely to be past its sell-by date by the time it is published. As a researcher working in the field, I know how hard it is to keep up.

3. **Lack of longitudinal studies:** To gain a better picture of how something has changed someone we need more than a snapshot. Just as we can't tell the impact that a child's schooling will have on them until they have fully grown up, we can't know how the Internet affects us until we all grow up. We need more than a snapshot. We need to study change over a long period. In thirty years' time we will have a better understanding of how those who were born at the start of the smartphone revolution are different (or not) from those born just before it. Given the relative newness of the Internet, there are few longitudinal studies currently available that are likely to stand the test of time.

4. **Lots of correlation, not much causation:** Where the research seems to be telling us something, it is often based on correlating two trends (like worsening mental health and increased use of smartphones) rather than causation – a provable link between the two. The problem with correlation is that it can lead us into the trap of becoming deterministic. Findings not presented with caution and due regard to their limitations can lead us to believe that because certain technologies exist, certain outcomes are inevitable. It is not helpful to view the Internet through such a deterministic lens, as this somewhat undermines the importance of character.

5. Not enough qualitative research: Most of what we think we know about the effect of the Internet on childhood is taken from data collected through questionnaires. These often-large-scale questionnaires or surveys are a good way to map when children and young people use the Internet. They can show patterns about how and when they access it. This data can be combined with the vast data sets that Internet providers and others keep to give us very accurate records about use and how this changes over time. Questionnaires can also show how many times children think they have been bullied online (or indeed been the bully) or encountered material deemed inappropriate for their age. This is all useful but limited data. It does not show us how our children will interpret the materials they encounter online or what impact these will have on their moral, or indeed social development. What we need is more and better qualitative data to help us really see close up what is going on. Collecting good qualitative data is hard, as we need to track our children's every use of the Internet (a challenge in itself) and observe closely how this appears to be affecting them. Qualitative studies bring some complexity and nuance to larger-scale quantitative studies. There are just not enough of them currently being conducted.

6. Self-report delusional bias: Most studies rely on what children tell us about their use of the Internet. As any adult will know, it is wise to take what teenagers tell us about their lives with a pinch of salt. They might not intend to give false accounts but do so for reasons well known in research, such as being self-delusional or biased. Think about when the doctor asks you how much you drink, smoke and exercise. Perhaps, most importantly, if I can't say how I think my smartphone is affecting me, can I really expect the children I interview to give an accurate account?

Why we need the REACT and THRIVE models

Given the limitations outlined above, current research provides a mixed and messy picture about how technologies impact on morality. Interpretations of the data oscillate between extremes; young people online are depicted as being either predominantly dishonest or truthful, compassionate or callous, selfish or selfless, altruistic or egotistical, cowardly or courageous, and acting with either vanity or humility. What is required is more research that seeks to join the studies up. Some have tried to undertake this work, but few have adopted the character-based moral theoretical lens that underpins this book.

It is perhaps not surprising that the research that has been undertaken is underutilised in practice. It has simply not given any us clear answers about *what to do*.

I believe we have to accept the limitations of the research, but not let this stop us seeking better data that will give us better ideas about how we can help our children thrive in their cyber-worlds. The way I propose doing this is by combining what we do know (taking into account the limits of our knowledge) with a theoretical position from which we can develop educational activities, and continue to carry out high-quality research.

It is this theoretical position, one that emphasises character and cyber-wisdom, that is central to the REACT and THRIVE models.

To parent today in the digital world we need some guiding principles. This is what the REACT and THRIVE models are all about. Although I would be the first to claim that the models outlined in this book won't solve all the challenges the Internet has thrown at us, my modest aspiration is to offer some guiding and structured principles to help you to parent and/or teach. I am introducing the models to expose current gaps and shape current and future thinking. The REACT and THRIVE models are designed to help parents and other educators think about what they currently do as well as what they might do differently.

They don't provide a step-by-step blueprint for parenting or teaching.

My hope is that they may provide a framework to think about how to respond to the cyber-revolution. They also provide the basis for taking practical action – possibly even changing how you parent and teach. The final chapter provides some educational ideas and activities, informed by virtue-ethical theory and the two models, that you might use with your children.

When you read through the background to the models, it is important you think about how best they can be applied to your own specific situation. You must use your own wisdom to shape your approach with an understanding of the unique natures of your own children.

The REACT model outlines the role we must play. REACT stands for:

Be a **R**ule-maker
Be an **E**xemplar
Be an **A**dvisor
Be a **C**haracter champion
Thrive.

The model aspires to help a new generation of parents to support, guide, model, advise and champion their children's wisdom and character. In turn, this will create a new generation of children possessing an inner cohesion, an ability to learn from joy and pain, and in doing so it will develop their cyber-virtues and cyber-wisdom. Children will be able to utilise the incredible power of the Internet to ensure that there is a greater chance of those around them, as well as themselves, thriving.

The THRIVE model stands for the six qualities we should seek to cultivate in our children to help them flourish in their digital worlds. THRIVE stands for:

Be **T**houghtful
Be **H**uman
Be **R**eason**ABLE**
Have **I**ntegrity
Be **V**irtuous
Be an **E**xemplar

To thrive is to blossom. It is also a hard, ongoing but ultimately fulfilling developmental journey. Our job is to help our children undertake this journey.

In the next two parts I will go into much more detail about each of the components in the REACT and THRIVE models.

Activity: REACT and THRIVE

Answer the questions below to see what components of the REACT model you already prioritise and which you might need to work on more.

How good do you think you currently are at . . .?

- making rules for your children's use of technology and upholding them?
  Very Good / Good / Okay / Poor / Very Poor

- being an exemplar to your children?
  Very Good / Good / Okay / Poor / Very Poor

- advising your children about their lives in the cyber-world, but letting them take the lead?
  Very Good / Good / Okay / Poor / Very Poor

- championing your children's character and stepping in when they don't show the best of themselves online?
  Very Good / Good / Okay / Poor / Very Poor

- focusing on your children's long-term thriving rather than their shorter-term daily online concerns?
  Very Good / Good / Okay / Poor / Very Poor

Now answer the questions below to see what components of the THRIVE model your children currently prioritise in their online lives.

How good do you think your children currently are at . . .?

- being thoughtful in their online interactions?
  Very Good / Good / Okay / Poor / Very Poor

- being FULL of thoughts in their online interactions – reflecting on what they do online?
  Very Good / Good / Okay / Poor / Very Poor

- recognising and understanding the difference between their qualities as a human and the qualities of the technologies they own?
  Very Good / Good / Okay / Poor / Very Poor

- pausing and thinking through the different dilemmas they face online, and using their judgement and reasoning to decide on the best course of action?
  Very Good / Good / Okay / Poor / Very Poor

- having a vision for, and trying to live up to, a life of integrity online?
  Very Good / Good / Okay / Poor / Very Poor

- trying to show virtue in everything they do online?
  Very Good / Good / Okay / Poor / Very Poor

- being an exemplar to others – both online and offline.
Very Good / Good / Okay / Poor / Very Poor

Your answers to these questions will provide you with a guide as to which chapters in Parts Two and Three you most need to focus on.

CHAPTER 5: KEY MESSAGES

- We need models to help us parent better in the twenty-first century, as many of the challenges that cyber-technologies have brought with them are new. We can't always turn to the past for advice on what to do.

- Research into the effects that cyber-technologies have on children's morals and ethics is currently impoverished – research in this area suffers from many limitations.

- If we want to act now to counter online concerns, we must turn to theory to fill the gaps left by the research.

- REACT and THRIVE are theoretical models that provide a framework for educating for cyber-flourishing.

- The components of REACT are: be a **R**ule-maker, **E**xemplar, **A**dvisor and **C**haracter champion to help your children **T**hrive online. These are the qualities educators need to develop.

- The components of the THRIVE model are: Be **T**houghtful, Be **H**uman, Be **R**easonABLE, Have **I**ntegrity, Be **V**irtuous, Be an **E**xemplar. These are the qualities children need to develop.

Summary of Part One: Flourishing Online

I have written this book in the hope that it will inspire some of you to think differently. I have also written it because I feel, as a parent, it is my responsibility to know everything I can that will help my children to flourish, not just in themselves but as part of a wider and increasingly connected society.

One of the biggest concerns I have for my children is how they will navigate the cyber-worlds they have just entered. I have found that some of my concerns are well founded, but that they are perhaps overly pessimistic. The Internet, as I have found out first-hand, affords our children some spectacular opportunities, ones that they can embrace not only to change their own worlds for the better but also to improve the worlds of others.

What choices they make, the path they follow, depends on their character and their wisdom.

I hope that the key messages in this part of the book, summarised below, will serve as conversation starters for everyone who also has a responsibility for educating for character and cyber-wisdom:

- we are sleepwalking into a state of technological determinism (losing control). We have forgotten that how we use the Internet depends on our character;

- we have an overly optimistic hope that governments and Big Tech companies will regulate the Internet so that bad things don't happen to our children;

- we must take the responsibility for cyber-flourishing into our own hands by actively seeking to educate our children to be able to navigate their cyber-worlds successfully;

- we must, therefore, seek to develop in our children technological knowledge about how to use computers in equal measure to practical ethical knowledge about how to use them wisely;

- we have to work together and be intentional, planned and reflective in our approach to building character and cyber-wisdom in our children.

The REACT and THRIVE models show how we can help our children not just survive in the cyber-world but thrive in it.

Part Two

REACT

6
Why REACT?

The journey from rules to thriving – via character

Part One of this book has been about what character and cyber-wisdom are and why these qualities are important. The remainder of the book answers a different question: how do we cultivate character and cyber-wisdom in children and young people?

In Part Two, I provide a detailed overview of each of the components in the REACT model. Although I deal with each component individually (one chapter for each), the five components are not meant to be viewed independently. They flow from one to another – they are a developmental journey from rules to thriving.

My advice is not to focus on one component at a time and move on to the next once you've mastered it. It is more complex than that. Initially, all of the components will most likely be in play at the same time. We need to be constantly attending to them all. However, at different times in our children's development, some might come into sharper focus. The aspiration is that as our children move from rules to character, some of the components become obsolete.

The ideal is that if our children are routinely making wise decisions, there is no need for rules. The ideal is that they are thriving online due to their own enhanced cyber-wisdom.

Reacting the right way at the right time

Before turning to the individual components of the REACT model, I need to say something about why I have deliberately chosen REACT as the acronym for the model. This is important.

Technology is not going to stop advancing and it will continue to change how we live. We need to learn how to react to new innovations in the right way to ensure they are used in a manner that maximises the common good. This is true of the Internet. It exists and most of our children choose to interact with it. They must learn how to respond to its constant presence in their lives, to learn how to use it well and how to use it wisely. They have to learn how best to respond to its demands and counter those that are likely to have negative consequences. This reaction might, of course, include ignoring the cyber-world as much as they can – literally switching it off.

Putting this more simply, I believe we can help our children thrive online if we can help them react in the right way to the cyber-technologies they possess and regularly use.

This puts the focus squarely on the human agency of our children. Having agency is to have the capacity to act independently, to make choices and decisions freely. It requires our children to be discerning when making judgements. To have agency is to have the freedom to think, reason, decide and choose on a course of action when presented with an issue or dilemma.

It is to react well or in the 'right' way when online. In other words, to possess cyber-wisdom.

It is not to react because one is following a rule, or because one is worried about the consequences of one's actions. It is to react showing justice, courage, care, honesty or whatever human quality the situation demands. The REACT model is therefore a rejection of technological determinism. It is about all of us having the freedom to choose how we use technology and for what purpose.

We may not be in full command of the means, but we do have a say on the ends.

Of course, some of you might want to argue that it is better to *act* than to *react*. I use the term react as it might be considered less spontaneous. To react, for me, is to take some time to think before doing. To act is to sometimes miss out the thinking and get straight to the doing.

Think about how your children might respond when they are sent a message via social media that they think is unfair. If they *act* immediately, in the heat of the moment, they might send a message back that is rash and ill thought through. To act spontaneously is often to act in a way that is driven by negative emotions such as anger. In these situations, we often draw on unconscious biases and stored-up prejudices.

Far better for our children to *react* to the message having taken some time to think through the alternative courses of action. To pause. To think, *Why is the message upsetting me?* Could they have taken it out of context? Is what they think the message means definitely what the sender intended it to mean? What is the likely consequence if they send an angry message back?

We need to help our children react after pausing and taking some time to think. We need to help them learn to think calmly and with clarity. This requires them to engage the brain alongside their emotions. It might require them to go on a fact-finding mission looking for evidence about what would be the best course of action. It will require them to reason and use their experience and logic to respond well. This might mean, in some cases, not responding at all.

It is about how our children react when they are first given a smartphone and Wi-Fi access. It is about how they react when they are playing an online game and they notice other competitors being cruel to each other. It is about how they react when they first sign up for a social media account and set up an online profile. It is about how they react when they are sent a post that encourages them to bully someone else in their class. It is about how they react when their friend sends them an inappropriate picture and asks them to send it on.

If they react well in these situations, our children will live happier lives online.

Developing good habits

To be able to react well requires freedom. It is about individual choice, not about being told how to behave. This does not mean that children don't need our help. This is where we come in, as parents and educators. Our job is to put up the scaffolding that will help them make decisions about how to react or what to say when they get drawn into a bullying conversation on Snapchat. We then need to know when to start taking down the scaffolding and trusting our children to stand up alone. It is the tension between our children's freedom in the cyber-world and our role to help them navigate it that is at the heart of the REACT model.

It is in the interests of the makers of the technology to grab and hold our children's attention. Sometimes this pulls them in a direction that will go against their better nature. This is why we need to build courage and judgement in our children. Are they able to show restraint when they know all their friends are online? Are they able to act with honesty and be accountable rather than post items online anonymously? Are they able to resist the temptation to send to others posts they know will hurt?

We need to help our children to understand that they are ultimately in control of their smartphones, laptops, gaming machines and computers. They have the choice when to use these technologies, and for what purpose. We also need our children to zoom out from the day-to-day interactions in their cyber-worlds and think more generally about how they can react to the technology to improve their cyber-worlds. Look more at the macro than the micro. This is about choosing and using technology that enhances rather than diminishes humanity.

The ultimate aim is to move from conscious to unconscious positive reactions. This means to take actions that are not hot-headed or based on biases, but are the habitual display of cyber-wisdom. Good habits are formed through repeated good (re)actions. Through experience and reflection. With support of good mentoring and coaching. Building good habits is likely to involve a process of getting things wrong and learning from the experience. This process takes time and will often be painful.

It is rare to find someone who is fully habituated into positive reactions – who always, without thought or deliberation, makes the right call. This is perhaps even more rare in the cyber-world, where new technologies come into all our lives at such a pace that we constantly having to adjust, think and learn again about how best to react to their presence in our lives.

When does the REACT model become relevant to me?

A question that might rightly be asked is when should the REACT model kick in? There is no correct answer to this question as it depends on the developmental stage of your children and when they are first exposed to cyber-technologies. The model, as previously stated, becomes relevant when your children start to use cyber-technologies that are interactive. It is also when they have their own device that they can use largely independently. For most children this will be when they own their first smartphone, laptop or tablet.

This is perhaps one of the harder decisions for a parent – when should you buy your child a (smart)phone? A few years ago, the norm seemed to be that you bought your child a smartphone when they went to secondary school at around the age of eleven. But my observation is that this is changing. My daughter tells me that only her and her friend did not have a phone in her class in the final year of primary school. My son, who is nine, says that many of his friends have phones, as do some children in the years below.

I watched my friends' children use their phones. It was clear that they were being used in different ways. Some had their phones out all the time, others rarely. Some had access to hundreds of apps, others could only use their phones for texts and calls. Some had the very latest iPhone, others a retro Nokia where the game 'Snake' held their attention. The point is it is not so much when you give your child a phone or iPad or computer, as what they use it for, that matters.

The model is not, therefore, relevant to a toddler watching television on an iPad, although I believe the first component, to be a rule-maker, is important at this stage. For me, the model became relevant when my daughter got her first mobile phone, because:

- this was when she had the freedom and potential to go anywhere from the comfort of her bedroom;

- this was when her character was tested through her digital interactions;

- this was when we first sat down together and co-constructed some ground rules for its use;

- this was when I felt it was most important for me to be aware of my own smartphone use, what I was exemplifying. How could I advise her authentically, if she could see I was not following my own guidance?

- this was when my daughter sought advice as she learnt to use the phone. I used these openings to talk not just about technology but also about character. My advice related to the real-life dramas and dilemmas of her cyber-world.

My focus on her character has been something I have undertaken implicitly and explicitly since she was born. Now the focus was on her character in the cyber-world – how she negotiated new and different risks and opportunities.

For me, the REACT model kicked in when my daughter was eleven years old. For you, it might be earlier or later.

CHAPTER 6: KEY MESSAGES

- The technologies we worry about are not going away, therefore we must help our children react in the right way at the right time when online.

- The more our children learn to react well in different circumstances, the more likely they are to develop habits of character that will serve them well online. The more likely they are also to develop cyber-wisdom.

- The REACT model will kick in at different times for different parents and children. It is most pertinent when children start interacting with others online.

7

Be a Ground-rule-maker

Steve Jobs, the co-founder of Apple, famously limited his own children's use of the technology he helped to invent. He recognised that it was not all good. He might well have subscribed to the age-old saying 'everything is good in moderation'. As parents, we also have to decide how much we allow our children to use their phones, tablets and Internet-enabled computers. Teachers need to decide policies on phone use in schools. It requires us to make rules that establish boundaries for our children's use of technology. This is no easy task. It is a necessary one.

Many parents worry about the amount of screen-time our children are being exposed to. This worry is driven by a number of concerns. Nostalgia, I think, is chief among them. We think back to our own childhoods when technology was not so prevalent. We think it would be healthier for our children to be outside playing and soaking up the fresh air. These dreamy thoughts can be quickly broken by our children asking us to buy them a new device, or begging permission to download a new app or play a video game. Making decisions about rules in such an environment is not easy. However, the road to character requires some ground rules. The good news is that if you start the journey well, your children are more likely to develop qualities that will eventually make rules obsolete.

The road to character starts with rules. Or, as I prefer to call them, ground rules. These are the boundaries, duties and expectations that we must lay down for our children from the outset. They are the foundations for what is to come. What makes the situation hard for us is that there are no right or wrong rules. There is no blueprint. There is no universal code of conduct that we can take off the shelf and apply in our homes or indeed schools. We have to rely on our judgement, knowledge and, at times, instinct, when constructing our bespoke version of the ground rules. I do, however, make some suggestions in this chapter on rules you might adopt and adapt to get you started.

Adults have been making rules for children since the beginning of time. In more recent times, our parents had to make decisions about how much television we should be watching and what computer games we could play. As our parents made rules about technology access and appropriate content for us, we must do the same for our children. However, it is harder for us. When we were growing up, most of us had access to television with a few channels and perhaps even games machines like the Sega and Nintendo. Our children today have access to a much greater array of technology and all of it affords them much greater freedom. The risks of us not establishing and upholding rules are therefore greater.

Facebook and other Big Tech companies are aware of these dangers and this is why they set rules themselves. For example, you are breaking their rules if you use Facebook before you are thirteen years old. The company states this policy in pretty blunt terms. They say:

> Facebook requires everyone to be at least *13 years old* before they can create an account (in some jurisdictions, this age limit may be higher). Creating an account with false info is a violation of our terms. This includes accounts registered on the behalf of someone under 13.[1]

However, until recently many children under the age of thirteen had a Facebook account or knew someone who did. These days Facebook is not as popular with children, but the same issues apply. It is very difficult for companies like Facebook to verify if a user is thirteen years old, so the rules are not enforced and are often bypassed at will.

We can't leave it to companies or indeed governments to construct and enforce rules. We must take this responsibility on ourselves. How successful we are at this, like so many other parenting tasks, comes down to trial and error. The rules we construct will no doubt be under constant review and will require regular renegotiation. Our children will also not always follow them.

The whole process of making and enforcing rules should be natural. My children have had rules and boundaries enforced upon them since they were born. I told my young children what they should and should not be eating, not to poke their fingers in the electric sockets, where they could and could not go. Most of us do this as second nature. Making rules that apply to our children's use of technologies is somewhat different. First, the rules we enforce on our children in the early years are normally linked to keeping them healthy and safe. The risks associated with different technologies are more opaque – we can't predict what the outcome will be of our sons and daughters using their smartphones after they are supposed to have gone to bed. And we can't look to our parents for inspiration.

This chapter helps you to consider how you should make your own rules. It will help you think about what rules will work for you and your children. It starts by considering what rules you might put in place and then moves to how you might monitor and enforce these. Even if your children don't thank you at first for making the rules and then enforcing them, I believe they will do so in time.

What ground rules?

In 2019 the then UK Chief Medical Officer, Dame Sally Davies, issued guidance on screen-time. What made this advice interesting was that much of it was aimed at families, not just children. This is an important point and one made by organisations such as Parentszone[2] – an organisation that helps families live successfully in the digital world. Rules and boundaries often work best when they are shared by everyone in the house. This is why the E of the REACT model is to be an exemplar. Following certain rules, such as not using phones at bedtime, is a way of setting an example to our children. Whenever 'rules' such as these are suggested by policy makers, they are hotly debated. Debates on the issue are also a popular topic on parenting websites.

It is relatively easy to establish rules that seek to limit screen-time, but making rules to restrict content is harder. I sometimes seek advice about what I should be stopping my children accessing through the Internet. In the same way that I can check the British Film Board's classification of films, I can look up advice on websites such as Common Sense Media[3] to see what is and is not appropriate for our children to consume online. However, websites that classify content tend to give advice on well-known traditional media such as films and TV shows, whereas there is so much more than that available online. Just think how many videos our children can watch on YouTube. Not all of these can be classified, but we know some are positive, such as the ones my daughter watches to help her with her maths homework, and others are, well, just not so *good*. There is also so much content online, which makes our job – to construct and enforce rules – so much harder.

Given this challenge, the lack of evidence about 'what works' and the considerable debates among parents on the topic of rules, I am not going to suggest a hard-and-fast set of (ground) rules that all adults should implement. As I have said, I don't think such a set of universal rules is desirable or indeed enforceable. Instead, I provide below some ideas for what ground rules you might establish. These are not a blueprint for parenting in the digital age. They are designed to inspire and inform. You know your children best and you need to decide which ground rules will work for you and your family.

First, I suggest some rules for reducing or stopping the use of cyber-technologies by children; then I give some advice on monitoring these rules.

Making the rules

In 2019, research showed that we spend more time – an average of thirty minutes more each day – at home with our families than we did twenty years ago.[4] This, for many, might seem like a good thing. It is, however, probably not a coincidence that the timing of the increase coincides with the invention of the smartphone. So, although we might spend more time at home, we may actually be spending less time at home interacting face to face with our families. This is what the prominent Professor of Social Science Sherry Turkle[5] called 'alone together' in her popular 2013 TED talk. Every year, Ofcom statistics show that we spend more and more time online. In 2018, adults spent on average three hours and fifteen minutes online each day – eleven minutes more than in 2017. That equates to a staggering fifty days a year.[6]

The science on the impact of screen-time on our children or indeed any of us is hotly debated. I have read through much of the research and the following reasons alone convince me that parents should be putting some limits on screen-time:

- Gaming disorder is now recognised by the World Health Organization (WHO) as concern grows for the number of children addicted to playing games online.

- Many studies show that human connection is vital for human happiness and flourishing – spending too much time alone online is likely to negatively affect our sense of wellbeing and mental health.

- The more time children spend online the more likely they are to discover apps/games and other cyber-software that have a negative rather than positive impact on their character development. This is more about content than screen-time, but the two are related.

You will no doubt have other reasons for limiting screen-time and the content your children access that align with your values and principles.

Here are some suggestions for rules you might make to help your children learn to use their cyber-technologies more wisely and establish firm foundations for character to be built upon.

Making meals a mobile-free time

For generations, parenting experts have lamented the loss of the family mealtime. For some, this is harking back to the 'good old days', but many schools I visit now enforce a 'family lunchtime', in which children and teachers sit and talk together as they eat. In one school I have visited, the whole process is directed – a topic of discussion is decided upon, and the conversation must be reported back afterwards.

I believe that mealtimes should be natural, but are a good time to catch up with the family. If we are all looking at devices when we eat, this opportunity might be lost. Jordan Shapiro disagrees. He has cautioned against a blanket ban on phones at mealtimes, as he says they can actually help aid family dialogue. An example he gives is checking something on Google to start or continue a conversation. He comments: 'I agree we shouldn't be watching YouTube at the table, but what about when you need to Google something which might enrich the discussion you're having? I'd say that enhances the experience.'[7]

The rule you make around using mobiles at mealtimes is up to you. My argument is that they should only be used if they enhance face-to-face interaction between us and our children. Mealtimes are important times to learn from our children about their day, what they are happy about, what is troubling them. It creates stronger bonds between us.

I treasure family mealtimes. I will encourage my children to check something online if it enhances our conversation. But, primarily, I hope that mealtimes will be a chance to check in with my children, to find out what sort of day they have had. This is when I learn about their lives, and this knowledge is essential if I am able to fulfil the A of the REACT model. To act as their advisor and supporter.

Bedrooms as a mobile-free space

A recent Childwise survey found that 50 per cent of children say they sleep with their mobile phone beside their bed.[8] We don't need research to tell us that mobile phones in the bedroom interrupt sleep – just ask any teacher. I have and they tell me of the tired faces that often meet them at the start of each day. The science of sleep is an evolving field, but there are well-established links between sleep and mental and physical health.

I have a simple answer to this: make bedrooms a mobile-free space after a certain time each day. This goes for me as well. I leave my phone in the corridor before I head to bed. It stops me getting stuck down a rabbit hole when I check something just before I am about to go to sleep. It will stop your children getting caught up in an online chat where they might, when tired, say something they will regret when they wake up.

Cyber-free headspace

The Internet has not been a friend to the great procrastinators of the world. No one who knows me would describe me as a procrastinator, but even I have decided to hide my phone when writing this book – it is just too distracting if it is next to me. The urge to pick it up and check for emails, or see what's happening in the news, is simply too great. If it is out of sight, it is out of mind. This is one of the reasons I like flying; I am forced to put the cyber-world behind me (at least until Wi-Fi on planes becomes standard).

Just turning off the notifications is not enough – it is the proximity that counts. The issue is that these days, mobile phones do so much; they are our calculators and have other useful tools we need to complete tasks. Some schools encourage children to use phones to complete their homework.

If, in discussion with your child, you see their mobile is distracting them, it might be time to reduce the use of their phone and buy a calculator. There are even apps that can help you do this, such as Our Pact,[9] which you can set to allow, say, ninety minutes a day on platforms such as Instagram or Facebook. If your children are savvy enough to work out how to disable this app, then parents get a notification.

You might go a step further and insist on silence. In Erling Kagge's excellent short but poignant book on silence, he describes how he tried to convince his three daughters that the world's secrets are hidden in silence.[10] He explains how they resist this idea as their worlds are so noisy and much of this noise comes from their mobile phones. This noise is not just from the pings and rings as new messages appear, but also the noise in our heads as we process these messages. Kagge suggests that we need to encourage our children to sit through boredom. This is hard, but at the other side of boredom is where we start to truly feel and see purpose and it can also lead to creativity. Based on this idea, one rule might be to impose a period of silence once a week for the whole family. This is not just a ban on phones, but a ban on everything except sitting and listening. This might be seen as a form of meditation or mindfulness, and in the calmness we might learn that we can live without the distractions and find a richer inner peace.

Tech-free Tuesdays

It is good for our children to seek out opportunities to try different things and be creative. One way of ensuring this is to ban the use of all Internet-enabled technology on one day of the week. If it is a school day, then the rule should kick in before and after school. During this time, our children (and us) will be forced to seek out other forms of entertainment. We will be forced to explore and discover other ways to stay occupied. We might get bored and have to learn to deal with it. Tech-free days will not kill you or your children, but they might help you and them discover different ways of living.

Sharing screens

Rules are not all about banning digital technology; they can also be about how we use them. Professor Sonia Livingstone stresses the importance of sharing screens. This means that the technology is not isolating, but brings us together. Livingstone recommends that we not only watch things together, but also spend an hour a week sharing what we have watched or enjoyed online alone. She stresses that this helps make communication about digital technologies positive rather than negative.

Monitoring the rules

Rules without enforcement are likely to fail. This is why monitoring is essential.

The good news is that technology can be part of the solution. The bad news is that there is an array of solutions on offer and you have to make the decision concerning how much of a Big Brother you want or need to be. You could choose to monitor with a very light touch, relying on a significant amount of trust in your children; or you might go to the other extreme and keep a log of everything your children do online. Most of us will probably be somewhere in the middle.

The use of technological solutions to monitor the rules should come with a warning. They cannot be relied on; children find ways to get around them. A recent news story charted a rise in children buying so-called 'burner' phones that their parents don't know about. Another news story explained how children found it easy to get around restrictions placed on phone use by parents. Common ploys included changing the device's time setting to avoid downtime, deleting and reloading apps to bypass time limits, and buying software that bypasses parents' passcodes.

Technology solutions

There are a number of technologies available that allow us to track and monitor our children's use of their phone. I will introduce a few below, but the best app in the world for this purpose is . . . us. Using an app might give us some peace of mind, but it could also give us a false sense of security. Nothing can replace us carefully watching and responding to the needs of our children as they grow up in the cyber-world. We are the best app available on the market for this job. Others include:

Apple Screen Time: The screen-time feature on newer Apple iPhones allows you to see how much time your children are spending on their iPhones and on which apps. It also enables you to set up restrictions, downtime and limits on the use of different apps – such as social media or games.

mSpy: Tracks what calls and texts your children make as well as what apps they use.

Bark: Alerts you if it thinks your children have received messages that might be cyber-bullying or concerning for other reasons. Using algorithms, it monitors text messages, YouTube, emails and social networks for potential safety concerns.

Mobicip: Blocks sites you don't want your children to access, such as porn, gambling and others.

These are just a few examples – there are many others, as helping parents monitor the technology use of their children is big business.

Before you investigate and install these apps, there are three big questions to ask.

Should we use these apps without our children's knowledge?

I don't think we should. Helping our children to build character is about helping them to grow and develop independently – to become better at making wise decisions. This means we have to trust them. This will start with talking with your children about the types of apps you are using to monitor their use of technology. This is a conversation starter. It is a chance to discuss the potential risks of being online and what each person's concerns are. Ideally, you will agree on which apps are appropriate. If there is a disagreement, it is a chance for you to explain why you think some are appropriate and others aren't. Having such conversations is likely to build understanding and trust with your children. I would also argue it is less likely they will find ways to get around monitoring, such as buying or borrowing phones you don't know about.

How restrictive should we make our monitoring?

Most apps allow for different levels of monitoring, from being able to effectively mirror the phone and follow everything to more light-touch options. The answer to this question is likely to depend on how old your child is and, knowing their character and personality, what risks they are likely to be exposed to online.

When should you start switching off the monitoring?

I believe you must agree with your children when is the best time to allow your children to 'go it alone'. This will depend on you calculating the risks they will be exposed to, the maturity of your children and the level of cyber-wisdom they have developed.

Parent filters

Most Internet providers offer technology that allows you to block access to particular content. For example, the BT parental filter can restrict access to websites that host pornography, obscene and tasteless material, hate and self-harm, drugs, alcohol and tobacco, dating sites, nudity, weapons and violence, gambling, social networking, fashion and beauty, file sharing, games, media streaming and even all search engines. The blocker allows you to set different levels of restrictions from light to strict as well as the times it is activated. This tool, and others like it, are clearly useful for parents to use to restrict access to material they deem unsuitable for their children. Some might believe this to be overly paternalistic, but I don't see it as any different from the British Board of Film Classification issuing ratings for the appropriateness of films and video games, as mentioned earlier. These are judgements on what is and what is not suitable for our children. It provides evidence for parents to make wider decisions about what content is suitable for children to access.

The excellent organisation Common Sense Media[11] is a great source of advice on appropriate content. It also offers tutorials on how to put parental filters on different devices. If you visit its website, you can get information about the content of different films, TV programmes and games that will help you make decisions about which you should restrict access to at different ages. You ultimately decide if your children should access the content, but at least you have the information. Unfortunately, standard parent filters are not so useful, as they don't provide detail about specific online content, but allow you, instead, to blanket-ban sites hosting things that parents might feel are inappropriate.

I use the parental control features of my broadband supplier, as it brings me some peace of mind. However, I am very aware that it has limits and can only be temporary – my children are not going to live in a world where they will always have their content filtered. They also only have to leave the house to get around the filters. We cannot be reliant on the tech firms, technology itself or government regulation to restrict our children's access to sites. This is why, although we should welcome and use parental filters, we must also seek to hone wisdom in our children so that they themselves can be critically aware of the risks.

Why rules are insufficient on their own

Although rules are important, they are insufficient.

Many of the young people that I interviewed in my research felt they had more freedom online. The children and young people I spoke to felt they could behave online in a way they could not offline, and this meant, on occasion, breaking the rules. Most social media sites, for example, require children to be at least thirteen years old to use them, but, as I previously mentioned, children in countries across the world break this rule and have profiles on Facebook, Instagram and other such sites. To some extent this can be contagious; if a child sees their friend 'get away with it', they are more likely to do it themselves, particularly if they don't want to miss out.

Rules in real life are often perceived by parents to be enforced to a greater extent than rules in the cyber-world. John Suler, a professor of psychology, was one of the first people to write about why people might behave differently online compared to when they are offline. He called his theory the 'online dishabituation effect'.[12] Although he acknowledged the situation was complex, Suler believed this effect could be either benign or toxic. Benign effects are when people use features of the Internet to be more kind or generous or to help others anonymously. Toxic effects are when people use the Internet to harm or hurt others.

One factor that made negative behaviour more likely was what Suler called 'dis-associative anonymity', where online users don't own their behaviour as they don't have an integrated online and offline identity. My research has shown that children and young people are often able to describe how their friends' and their own behaviour changes when they are online. They describe gaining a sense of moral disengagement on the unregulated web. Perhaps, acting under a pseudonym, they allow themselves to disassociate from reality and become part of the online worlds they inhabit. For many children, this gives them courage to go places and do things they might not do otherwise. Going online anonymously could be viewed as a deliberate attempt, by some, to avoid detection when they wish to break the rules or undertake an act that is not morally defensible.

The chance to be anonymous and therefore forgo accountability is attractive to many children, and it is not surprising that some app developers make it one of their main marketing features. You will probably all have heard of WhatsApp and Instagram, but what about the following apps, which are just as easily downloadable?

- Yubo – dubbed by some as Tinder for teenagers and easy to access anonymously.

- Whisper – where the creator promotes sharing secrets and meeting new people.

- Ask.fm – an app that allows users to ask strangers questions anonymously.

These are just a few examples; there are many others. The creators of these apps and others like them talk about the beneficial reasons for using them. However, as it is easy for our children to use them anonymously, how do we know who they are online with and how can we monitor what they are doing? The ability to remain anonymous online leads invariably to a lack of accountability. Rules make it clear what is acceptable in any given society. But if you think you can bypass certain rules, would you? For example, would you be more likely to speed on the motorway if you could drive anonymously and avoid being caught?

When rules are absent or easy to bypass, character and wisdom matter more than ever. Character, as I will explain later on, is what you do when no one is looking.

The freedom and affordances the Internet offers children and young people is one of the main reasons that imposing rules and regulations can only be one part of any educational strategy designed to develop young cyber-citizens. The rules we make and impose are only the first stage of a character-based approach to flourishing online. They are a necessary pre-stage, but no more than that. Our children grow up and we can't restrict, monitor and regulate them for ever.

Letting our children go . . . carefully

We need to think carefully how we move from rules to character – how we let our children go free. Research has shown that children respond better to rules if they think their parents are being fair and appropriate. This means outright bans might actually have long-term negative effects. Allowing fair access to cyber-technologies is important for moral reasoning. Once we trust our children to make wiser decisions on their own, we should start to reduce or rewrite the rules.

This means that we cannot cocoon our children or be overly restrictive. We can't be helicopter or snowplough parents, where we try to pre-empt and remove any perceived obstacles to our children's happiness. We must be realistic. Our children are most likely going to see things online that upset them. Our job is to make sure that early on in their lives as cyber-citizens we impose rules and restrictions that ensure this is not happening too often, and if it does, they know you are there to help them through it. This is a form of pre-arming. We warn children of the risks and threats, we take a calculated approach as to how much they should be exposed to at any particular age and offer strategies that will help them overcome the threat should they be exposed to it.

Adopting a proactive but permissive approach is the best way to build character and cyber-wisdom.

Rules, rules, rules: Me and my daughter

I found it hard to apply any rules when my daughter got her first phone. This was less about her and more about me. Although I had been writing and thinking about this book for some time, I lost confidence when it came to actually drawing up the rules. I went into some sort of paralysis; I did not know where to start. I probably over-thought it. I did not know if the rules we were agreeing to were overly restrictive or not restrictive enough? I knew, in theory, that it is easier to start with tighter rules and then reduce them as you go along. But knowing where to draw the first line in the sand, the first set of rules that provide the foundations, proved to be much harder in practice.

I had a second problem. I had told myself that, when I made the rules with my daughter, I would use it as an opportunity to impose some rules on my own use of technologies. I had started to notice that my screen-time had got out of hand. I was checking my emails more than ever, looking at the news or aimlessly tapping on apps when bored. I found the compulsion to continuously check my phone had crept up on me. It had become addictive without me realising. It was not having any obvious dramatic effect on myself or my family. However, deep down, I knew it was not doing me or those I loved any good. I was becoming increasingly concerned about the possible pernicious effects of my relationship with my phone.

I found it was one thing to tell myself that I would use the opportunity to impose some rules on myself and another to actually do so. I decided to give my daughter my old phone. With it went all the apps I used, including the email and news apps I had become so drawn to. I found this really hard. I did not want to give these up. I also signed up to most of the rules that we, as a family, agreed to. These included:

- No mobile phones in the bedroom from half an hour before going to sleep – a new charging station appeared in the corridor overnight.

- No mobile phones at mealtimes unless they were being used to aid the conversation.

- My daughter agreed to let my wife or me look through her phone at any time if we asked to. In reality, we rarely needed to.

- My wife and I would monitor my daughter's use of the phone and speak to her if we were concerned about it. We would not 'mirror' her phone to see the content of her messages, but we agreed we might do this at a later stage if things started to happen that we or she were worried about.

- My daughter was not allowed access to social media sites until she met the age restrictions. After a few months, we did let her use WhatsApp with careful monitoring.

- My daughter would tell us if there was anything that happened on her phone that she was worried about.

We also initially bought my daughter a fairly restrictive phone package, with low limits on data, texts and phone calls.

My daughter accepted and stuck to these rules. The main tension was that she saw having a phone as part of growing up and was worried that we might become more restrictive. She also wanted the rules to be similar to those that her friends were subject to. In the end, establishing and upholding the rules was a far less painful experience than it seemed at first. It also did me some lasting good.

CHAPTER 7: KEY MESSAGES

- Implementing some ground rules to help your children manage their use of cyber-technologies is necessary. They provide the foundations that character can be built upon.

- Children can find their way around the rules you implement even if you monitor them. Don't rely on rules alone.

- There is no blueprint or ready-made set of rules that we can take off the shelf and implement. The rules you draw up with your children should be bespoke, and should reflect their character and the context in which they are growing up.

- It is important to let your children go carefully: think about when to reduce or remove rules and let them play more freely in their cyber-worlds and learn from doing so.

8

Be an Exemplar

The road to character and cyber-wisdom starts with admiration and assimilation. In short, our children learn from what we say and from what we do.

How our children choose to use digital technologies is likely to be informed by how we use our phones, laptops and computers, and, of course, how their friends and those around them use these technologies. When we think of exemplars and role models, we often think of famous sports people, musicians and, increasingly these days, YouTube stars and other online influencers. These people do influence our children, but their everyday behaviour is more likely to be shaped by those closer to them.

Put simply: if we are cyber-wise and our children's friends are cyber-wise, then it is more likely our children will also be cyber-wise.

This process might be called character *caught*. The last part of this book is full of learning approaches and activities that might be called character *taught*. Character taught is a collection of intentional and explicit character-education strategies directed at helping our children develop the qualities required to thrive in the cyber-world. Although these serve an important purpose, it is insufficient to focus only on these strategies. Character is largely caught. Character develops over time and is mostly shaped, almost by osmosis, by the places we grow up in and the people we grow up with.

We catch character from interacting with others. We learn what virtues are more or less important in different situations. We watch and we learn. Our children watch and they learn.

Intentionally or not, those who surround our children are role models or exemplars. This includes their teachers, other adults they connect with, their friends and peers, and, of course, us – their parents.

We might be good or not-so-good role models, but we are always 'on' and always modelling a form of behaviour.

Nurture

The nature versus nurture debate has gone on for generations. It is a debate that I often have at home with my wife as we try to identify the different traits in our children and where they might have got them from. Almost everyone agrees that both nature and nurture have a part to play in how people develop. Even the most ardent nature advocates like Robert Plomin[1] agree that some of our character is shaped through our interactions with the world.

It makes sense that if we are brought up in environments where we are surrounded by people who show compassion, courage and honesty then we are more likely to develop these qualities ourselves. This is not always the case, but it is likely. If the majority of our children's friends are being kind, thoughtful and acting with integrity online, our children are more likely to act the same way. For example, research shows us that if we volunteer, our children are also more likely to volunteer.[2] There are, of course, no guarantees, but generations of research into the importance of nurture on development show that our upbringing matters. Growing up is a formative time. The people we grow up with leave their mark on who we are and become. Parents are the most important influence on our character in our early years, and this role shifts over time to teachers and to our peers and friends.

This is why in the THRIVE model the E also stands for exemplars. If we are to thrive, we need our children to be surrounded by people who are striving to show cyber-wisdom. This is what is required to enable both a short-term and a longer-term virtuous circle. The current generation will define the ethos and social norms of their children's cyber-worlds.

How we and others exemplify cyber-wisdom is therefore important. This is why, after ground rules have been established, the next area we must attend to is how we exemplify a healthy relationship with the cyber-technologies we use. As our children take their first steps into the cyber-world, they will be watching, learning and adjusting their behaviour because of us.

The new role models

Before the Internet it was more likely that children would learn about character expectations through those with whom they were in close proximity. The people they mix with face to face most days of their lives, such as the children they play with in the playground, and their parents, wider family and teachers. This has all changed. Some of our children are just as likely to spend time playing *Fortnite* with friends in China or America as they are playing football with their friends in the park. In fact, today there is a trend to not even play the games but watch other 'stars' play them on Twitch, YouTube or Facebook Live. In this situation, these 'stars' are literally acting as role models, as they are being studied closely by our children in the same way a famous footballer might be.

The people our children interact with online provide an example for how they might act in the cyber-world. This troubles many of us. The main reason, I think, is that these online 'friends' don't come round for tea. We don't seem them in the flesh, we can't see how they behave in 'real-life' situations. We don't know them and can't judge if we think they will be a good or bad influence on our children.

We might be tempted to view these online friendships as shallow, meaningless and morally problematic. However, there is no reason why they can't be just as deep, rich and important as any other 'normal' friendships. There is no reason why they can't also be friendships based on shared mutual virtues. For one thing, social media has injected a new dynamism into friendships; it has given our children new ways to connect and maintain relationships.

We can't let nostalgia lead us into a trap of thinking that all online friendships are bad. Like offline friends, some are likely to be good and others not so good. Our children's online friends can be just as good character role models as those they know from school. It is more about who our children choose to be friends with and whose behaviour they are learning from and being inspired by. Of course, many friendships occur in both the real and cyber-world; they are blended or hybrid. Here, technological extensions are likely simply to amplify the best or worst of offline friendships. The bottom line is that there is no reason why online friendships can't be excellent exemplars to our children.

What we tell our children every day without speaking

The saying goes that we get the politicians we deserve. This is also true of the cyber-world. We get the cyber-world we help to make.

It is how we act and behave online that will help determine how those who follow us do. One of the hardest questions to ask is: what do we tell our children every day without speaking? What messages do they get from us that we have not purposely tried to communicate? Put bluntly, if we prioritise scrolling Facebook or looking at our emails over a conversation with our children after school, what are we *telling* them? Our role as exemplars in the cyber-world matters. If our children see us online all the time then why would they not think it is okay for them to do the same? If we use our mobile during mealtimes, how can we tell them not to?

There is a growing field of research into the role of exemplars in character development. A lot of it focuses around what might be called the admiration/emulation debate.[3]

- Admiration might be explained as what inspires us to do the right thing. These are things or people who create in us a sense of awe. They move us. But this is only stage one. To be awed and moved does not lead us necessarily to 'do' something, to take some form of action.

- We also need emulation, in which we copy the actions of people we admire.

Admiration and emulation are therefore not a dichotomy, but more of a continuum in practice. A good exemplar should show us what to do and inspire us to actually do it.

When I ask adults about role models, they often focus on the moral greats – people like Gandhi, Nelson Mandela, Rosa Parks, Mother Teresa and Martin Luther King. These are no doubt great people, who lived challenging lives, and there is a great deal in them to admire. However, are their stories relatable and attainable to us or our children? Will we ever face the same challenges and obstacles these moral greats did? After all, none of the people listed above lived in the cyber-world.

Our lives and therefore our stories are likely to be very different. This is why it is even more important that we are careful about what we are exemplifying to our children. My research and that of others shows that many children, when asked, say that family members and predominantly mothers are their most important role models. This is good and bad news. The good news is that we do offer a relatable and attainable role model. The bad news is that this puts more pressure on us to 'get it right'.

Imperfect exemplars – more human and more honest

We often think of exemplars as perfect beacons of moral virtues. The great and the good who always seem to make the right decision to do the right thing even when it is hard to do so. However, no human in history is ever like that. No one has always made the right decision. To be human is to be fallible. This is a pretty good lesson for our children. After all, we want them to follow exemplars that they think are achievable, otherwise they are only going to end up disheartened. If we set the bar too high, our children are unlikely to follow in our footsteps and will become disillusioned.

This is to say that we should be natural in front of our children. We can't seek to airbrush or cleanse. There are, of course, times to hide things from them, but not all the time. This takes wisdom. When is and when is not the time to let our children into the secret that we are not perfect?

It is about finding the right balance. We must be intentional in our actions with a sense of how they are being interpreted by our children. We can't give them warts and all, all of the time. But some warts, some of the time, is good. It is good for our children to see us sometimes struggling 'to do the right thing'. This means sharing with our children the times we have made 'mistakes' online or times when we have seen something on social media that has upset us, and that has made us react badly.

The aim is to try to be 'thick' exemplars; doing our best despite the complexities of real life. Thin exemplars, by comparison, would be superficial and almost float through life. In these examplars, there is no substance for children to observe and learn from. They need to learn from our struggles.

I tell my children plenty of times I have got things wrong. For example, the time I really hurt someone through a misdirected email. I had asked my friend if I could stay with them overnight during a work trip. My friend replied to say that it was a busy time and their partner would rather I did not stay. I forwarded the email on to my wife, saying in no uncertain terms what I felt about my friend and their partner. But I had hit *reply* rather than *forward*. Seriously awkward. I did my best to make amends, but my relationship with my friend has never been the same. The only solace I can take is that it was a learning experience for me (I'm now so much more careful) and it can be a learning experience for my children. In recounting the story to them, I also discuss with my children how I 'got it wrong' and what I learnt from the situation.

Children are more likely to learn from a thick exemplar, as they have to critically engage, they are forced to think, they are not simply mindlessly intimating or mimicking. That is to say, we want our children to reflect on and revise their behaviour, if necessary, based on what they observe; not copy and paste it. This is the difference between them becoming like the exemplar and becoming like what the exemplar exemplifies. We need our children to view exemplars through their own lens, shaped by the facts of their own lives, to put their own stamp on them.

It is good sometimes for our children to see the grey areas. They can see the black and white lines on the page, but it is the space between these lines where the real learning takes place. Aesop's fables are full of black and white lines where the 'moral message' is pretty clear. But such tales are rarely realistic. We want our children to observe their role models going through struggles, having to try hard to make wiser decisions. These are the grey areas, and these are the areas in which we can have the best learning conversations with our children.

For example, my children often notice and mention the following to me:

- when I am on my mobile phone as they are trying to ask me something;

- when I appear distracted by something I have read on my emails that has troubled me;

- when I turn to my mobile phone as a distraction in any moment of boredom;

- when I am tempted to check a text message in a traffic jam;

- when I use my laptop to watch television in bed;

- when I walk down the road bumping into people when I'm texting;

- when I turn to Google to answer any question they ask.

Although these are not, in themselves, horrendously bad actions, each time I do them I am telling my children something. They are learning from me. I therefore can't ignore them. I try to use the times they challenge me as an opportunity to discuss with them how I struggle with my relationship with my phone or laptop. That they have features that draw me in, that it is a constant struggle to put them down. I think this is the most human way to deal with such situations, and children learn best when we are like this.

Experimentations with screen-time

My message throughout this book is that the effects of screen-time on character should not be an issue per se. To focus too much on screen-time might mean we miss the real issue: how and what children use their Internet-enabled devices for. For example, is the content they access shaping their character negatively, and are they spending too long in isolation online and missing out on character-building experiences? As I strive to be a better exemplar for my children, I believe it is good for me to be aware of my own screen-time – to be aware of what I am modelling. In an effort to be more consciously aware of how I use my iPhone, I turned on the inbuilt Screen Time app. This is what I learnt from doing so:

- Looking regularly at data that showed how much I used the phone did serve a useful purpose: it made me more aware of how I was using my phone. However, the irony of increasing my screen-time through monitoring my screen-time was not lost on me.

- I did not find the overall figure of the time I spent on my phone each day very useful. But the more I dug into the data, the more useful it became. It was good to get an idea of how long I spend on each app – but I think this raw data alone does not tell the full story of how my phone use is impacting those around me. The data showed that I use my email app for less time than the news, podcast, maps and other apps. However, I know that the email app distracts me from family and friends the most. If I did not rely on my intuition here, the raw screen-time data could mask this.

- The most striking data was the pickup data and what I went to first when I picked up the phone. This showed me that although I was not on the phone for very long, I was picking it up regularly and I would check my emails first. Being aware of this habit now makes me pause and think whenever I pick up my phone.

- Discussing the screen-time usage data with my children did serve as a good conversation starter. It was the basis for some useful chats about my own and their relationship with the Internet.

I can see how the Screen Time application (or similar features on other types of smartphones) might be helpful for parents to become more aware of how they are using the Internet – stark data can be arresting. For me, it was a good experiment, but I don't think it helped me become a better exemplar on its own. I think I still get the best guidance when I am truly able to listen to the comments made by my family and other people who I respect about how they observe me using my phone.

Near peers

As adults, we are not always the most important exemplars for our children; the people closer to their age are. Our influence starts to wane as early as when our children are four years old, when they start to socialise regularly with other children at school. As children grow up, their peers become the biggest influence on how they act and behave. We might call these the 'near peer influencers'. Think back to when you were growing up. Perhaps it was the friends from your street, class or school who often inspired or guided your actions. These days, 'near peers' are just as likely to live all over the world and exert their influence through the Internet.

The big question for us is how do we deal with near online peers who might be setting less than desirable examples for our children? It is very hard for us to stop our children being friends with particular children, and often we don't know who they are. But there are some things we can do if we are concerned about what our children's friends are exemplifying. For example, if one of my children's friends is bullying others on social media, I should encourage my children to tell me about this. I can then step in and warn them that their friend is not setting a good example and that they should resist being persuaded to follow them. I see my role here is to give my children the strength and courage to resist; to stay strong and stay true to their convictions.

Other steps we can take include:

- Asking our children questions about their online friends so we can try to get to know them. We can find out what qualities they are attracted to in them.

- Observing our children. If online friendships are negative, this is likely to show in our children's actions and behaviour.

- Asking our children, in a non-threatening way, to talk us through some of their online communication with their friend – talk us through what they like and don't like about them.

- Asking if you can be a player in an online game with their online friends, or observe your children as they play the game.

- Taking other steps that will help get your children to trust you so that they feel they can speak honestly to you concerning their fears about their relationships with particular friends.

Through conversations and observations, we can discover in what ways these online role models are influencing our children and step in if we deem it to be necessary. If we think online friendships are having a negative effect, it might be time to reintroduce some rules – such as restricting access to the Internet. Rules can help reset the situation.

CHAPTER 8: KEY MESSAGES

- Our children learn from what we say and from what we do – this is the same in the cyber-world.

- We must think carefully what we are telling our children every day, without speaking, about how best to live in the cyber-world.

- Parents are the most important role models in their children's early years. Over time, teachers, and then children's near and less near peers, become increasingly important.

- We should not strive to be unrealistic 'perfect' exemplars; children learn best when they see our human side – our own fallibilities.

- Today, the peers who influence our children's character are as likely to come from around the world as from down the road. Our role is to help our children observe and understand how these peers are influencing their behaviour.

9

Be an Advisor

As the rules fall away and our children become more independent, we must learn to trust them to use their cyber-technologies wisely. We should seek to become less of a rule-maker and more of an advisor.

As advisors we play a number of different roles, including:

- being a teacher – leading learning;

- being a guide – demonstrating and showing what is expected;

- being a coach – focusing on the here and now, and responding to changing circumstances;

- being a mentor – focusing on the future and long-term goals;

- being a supporter – cheering on from the sidelines.

The skill is in when to play each of the above roles. At times, we must advise in the role of a teacher and lead from the front, and at other times we need to give advice as a supporter and let our children take the lead.

What all of these advisory roles have in common is that they start with listening. Only when we know what is going on are we able adequately to teach, coach, mentor, guide and support. These advisory roles are also not about the enforcement of rules. To be an advisor is to work selflessly with your children on a goal that will make their lives better. To be an advisor is to have knowledge and wisdom, but to offer this in a way that is directed by the needs of your children. Advising is about working in partnership, not about being in power. It requires us to really listen, to enhance our own knowledge through learning, to try to show unlimited patience, to be understanding and to be courageous. It is not easy work.

Learning from experience

We must let our children go forth, experience and play in their cyber-worlds. Although there are times when we might want to restrict our children's use of their smartphones and gaming apps, they will only really learn through experiencing and trying things out.

Real advice about real events is better than hypothetical advice about hypothetical events. Such hypothetical musing does have a purpose: it offers a chance to try out different schools of thought *if* things happen. The real learning, though, only kicks in *when* they do. This calls for us to be courageous and let our children experiment knowing that we are behind them and with them. They must know we are on hand offering support, advice and guidance as if it were on tap.

The *New York Times* journalist David Brooks makes an argument in his book *The Second Mountain: The Quest for a Moral Life* that the experiences in life that seem to destroy us can actually be the foundations for growth.[1] We can all think of experiences that seemed hard at the time; the ones we felt we could not get over, could not come back from. These often turn out to be the greatest learning experiences. This is Brooks' contention. In his book, he meets many people who tell such a story. In all of these stories, the chance to learn and grow depended largely on the capacity of the individual for deep reflection, and on the love and support of those around them. Brooks states that 'while our educational system generally prepares us for climbing this or that mountain, your life is actually defined by how you make use of your moment of greatest adversity'.

This is a call to make use of the so-called teachable moment. It is about our children learning 'on the job'. Learning while experiencing true and real events. Such learning can't necessarily be planned in advance or detailed on a curriculum. It is spontaneous learning. Responsive learning. Vulnerable learning. This type of learning happens sometimes when our children least expect it and sometimes they may feel they can't cope with it.

When I have successfully come through an adverse and challenging situation and learnt from it, I have leant on people around me for help. These 'helpers' did not necessarily lead me out of the adverse situation or even show me the way out. They also did not tell me to ignore or forget it. They encouraged me to face the situation. To learn, I need people who will listen, challenge, I ask the right questions, offer the right amount of support, offer love, and offer up their wisdom based on their experience. They will mostly possess practical wisdom. These are the sort of people we need to be for our children.

If our children are unfortunate enough to suffer adversity, say by being a victim of cyber-bullying at their school, then we need to be there to help our children through this. We cannot always 'fix' the situation although our instinct might be to seek out the bully and reprimand them. This action might help in the short term, but it won't necessarily fix the situation in the long run. We need to help our children deal with the situation themselves and help them find the strength to stand up to the bully or report them to a teacher if appropriate. This, for many of us, might be the harder course of action, but it is the best one in the long run.

What might give us strength is that our children are learning how to cope and how to respond for themselves. They are honing their cyber-wisdom. This is deeper, more sustained learning than fixing the immediate situation. It should, if we play our role right, help our children become more resilient and better able to withstand future adversities.

Constructive learning

Don't just take my word for it. Learning from experience has been a pedagogical method endorsed by some of our greatest educational thinkers over the last century. Long gone are the days of didactic, one-way teaching. Most people today understand that education is a two-way process and it is at its best when it is real. The legendary educationalist John Dewey was one of the first to observe, back in the early 1900s, that children learn best through doing.[2] Dewey rejected education as a form of behaviourism. We can't teach people by simply filling them up with knowledge, for we learn best through the application of knowledge in real life. It comes from independent thought, discovery and, ultimately, gradually becoming more autonomous leaders of our own learning.

Dewey coined the term 'experiential learning' to describe this school of thought. Although this sounds normal these days, it was a pretty revolutionary idea at the time. Great thinkers who followed, including Jean Piaget and Lev Vygotsky, followed up on this idea with their own versions of what is commonly known today as constructivist theory. This theory prioritised social learning; people coming together to construct new meanings. It was based on the premise that knowledge and understanding are in a perpetual state of development and that what matters is context. This type of learning is crucial in the modern day, as we just don't know where technologies will take us and what impact they will have on individuals and society in the future. The context is constantly shifting and therefore we need to work together to construct new meanings.

The ideas of experiential and constructivist learning underpin an important aspect of what it means to be an advisor. Our role is to support and advise our children as they go out and discover, learn and reshape their own and other people's worlds. This is an easy, even joyful role when everything is going well and when our children are using technologies that bring them and other people pleasure. It is even more satisfying if this pleasure also improves society. But our role as an advisor really kicks in when things are not going so well. It is hard when we see our children struggling and upset. But it is also one of the most important times for learning.

Experiential learning in action: Online plagiarism

It is an old adage, but a true one, that we learn best in times of adversity. No one, though, wants to face adversity alone. We all want someone with us at these times, offering support and appropriate advice. This is my approach when one of my students is caught plagiarising, a troubling issue on the rise in many universities. It is a hard situation for my student to face, but my job is to help them learn from it. I could take regressive action and dock them marks or, in severe cases, make them retake the module. However, I would rather help them learn from the situation. It is often the case that students have made a mistake. Many come to universities unable to see that online plagiarism is wrong, especially as many have 'got away with it' at school. If something is good and can be easily copied from the Internet, then, they reason, why not use it?

As a teacher, I think my students can learn more about character and practical wisdom from this situation than in any lecture on these topics. It is in these moments I can help them understand, through questioning, why their actions have been immoral. They can learn what is and is not appropriate. I can see in my students' faces they hate this situation. They hate having to face up to what they have done. But after I've spent some time talking to them, they relax, start to think, and normally begin to respond in the ways I would hope. I am largely acting as an advisor rather than as an enforcer. I start out as a teacher in these meetings and end up as a coach and mentor. The students rarely commit the same mistake again. They have learnt from the adverse experience.

The important point I am making here is that we have to trust our children to play in the digital world, in full knowledge that they are likely to make mistakes. Of course, we can only be an advisor if our children allow us to be. We need them to trust us. We need to keep the lines of communication open. This requires us to be a partner as they learn to successfully navigate their cyber-worlds.

Building a partnership with our children

Experiential learning works when we build partnerships with our children. We need them to think that they can share with us the pain and joy of living in their cyber-worlds. This is much easier said than done. To build partnerships, both we and our children need to demonstrate some core virtues. The most important of these, I think, are honesty, openness, gratitude, patience, tolerance, compassion and courage.

If we are able to show these qualities, then we are more likely to be able to have vulnerable conversations in which we can share our fears and concerns. Our children can tell us if they have witnessed something on social media that is making them feel uneasy, and we are able to tell our children that we are concerned if we feel they are playing an online game for too long. These can be difficult conversations if the foundations for a solid partnership are not in place. Of course, these foundations are built from birth and nurtured as our children grow up. The partnership will also no doubt go through better and worse times, but the key is to keep the core virtues in place, to keep a shared sense of openness and trust.

At the heart of a good partnership is conversation. Conversation that allows for disagreement, discussion and debate. Conversation that is not one-sided but involves both parties having a voice and feeling free to give their opinion. In conversations with your children about the Internet, you are likely to experience a clash of values. For example, your child might feel they should use their smartphone more than you think they should, or that they consider something they posted online not to be offensive, when you think it is. Such clashes of values are likely to be commonplace in these conversations, as they are in any walk of life. What matters is that both parties in these conversations try to show some common virtues. If we and our children can try to remain honest, compassionate, courageous and tolerant, our conversations are likely to be better. We won't always agree, but we will feel better about agreeing to disagree. We will leave difficult conversations in a better place where they can be picked up again at a later stage. We should view a good conversation as central to any good partnership.

Research shows that bullying normally goes on when children are alone and not under the watchful eyes of others. Research has also shown that teachers and parents are often unaware of bullying, with one study showing that 90 per cent of young people do not tell their parents or other adults that they are being cyber-bullied.[3] My own research shows that it is particularly difficult for parents to monitor cyber-bullying because it occurs via so many different types of technology, including chatrooms, email, instant messaging, online blogs, social networking websites, role-playing games and video broadcasting websites. If we are to help our children when they fall victim to cyber-bullying, they must believe we are on their side; that we are in partnership with them. Advice is sought and given most successfully in situations when both parties feel as though they are working together in partnership.

I use the following approaches, more or less successfully, to try to build better partnerships with my children:

Keep talking: I try to grab any moment I can to keep the conversation going. This is usually at mealtimes, but also first thing in the morning or just before they go to bed. I want my children to feel they can talk to me at any time, and that I will listen and try to understand. Most of the time our talking is about seemingly unimportant things, but the simple act of talking is, for me, the most important thing. This will, I believe, ensure they feel they can talk to me when things get difficult.

Leaving them alone: I have tried to learn when my children need time alone for silence and reflection. Leaving my children alone, feeling safe, offers a good chance for them to think through things that have been troubling them. When they are ready to talk, I believe my job is to help them find the language so that they can tell me about what is troubling them.

Understand they always need love: However grumpy and moody my children are, they always need love. Often their grumpiness is actually a desperate call for more love and support. When they are moody, my innate reaction is to be moody back. It can take a real fight, against myself and my children, to give love in this situation. But if I can, the outcomes are always better.

Listening: I have a tendency to fill gaps to avoid silence. I am learning to listen to my children more. I am also getting better at trying to listen for the things they think they are trying to tell me, but not telling me. This requires me to listen harder. To listen between the gaps in their words. To listen by looking at their body language and expression. To ask questions to aid understanding and interpretation.

Trying to be non-judgemental: I try to let my children speak first and tell me what happened before judging. I am aware that when I judge a situation, I am giving away what I am thinking through my body language. I have to try hard to stay neutral until I know all the facts of the situation. When I remain non-judgemental, I know my children are more likely to tell me truthfully and in their own words their good and less good experiences of living in their cyber-worlds.

Learning alongside our children

To be an advisor we need to have some knowledge of what we are advising about. We do not necessarily have to be experts, but we do need to know enough of the language to be able to have conversations with our children about their lives in the cyber-world. We need to know what technologies they are talking about, what apps they use and what they use them for. We need to learn text speak and recognise emojis. We need to learn a new language.

As I called for in Part One of this book, we need to become digital immigrants. We should explore the cyber-world alongside our children and help them navigate the best and the worst of the Internet. We should be seeking to develop our own cyber-wisdom as we help our children develop theirs.

Some people call this process developing adult digital literacy. This is often taken to mean adults becoming more proficient using the technology – how to use its various functions. I am talking about much more than this. To be a digital immigrant is not just to learn the skills of how to use the technology; it is also to live in the cyber-world and form values, opinions about what impact the technology is having on individuals as well as society from first-hand experience. Living in the world is to know more and understand more. It is to try to shape the world based on this knowledge and experience. It is to pass down this knowledge and experience to our children.

Research by Vicky Goodyear and Kathy Armour shows just how much adults often 'don't get it'.[4] Goodyear and Armour contend that adults who don't try to engage and live with their children in their cyber-worlds might be storing up issues down the line. The children in Goodyear and Armour's research identified parents as key sources of support. However, many of these children also thought their parents were ignorant. They also found that children were resistant to talking to their parents about problems, out of fear of having their phones confiscated as they might not understand the issues. The children they spoke to called for adults to be better informed about the problems of the current generation.

To be a digital immigrant does not necessarily mean always being positive about cyber-technologies, but it does mean we should not be overly negative. Through understanding the risks of cyber-technologies, we can help ourselves and our children avoid them. They should not be ignored. But we should also not ignore opportunities to show our children the positive outcomes that can be gained from using them. This requires us to put in effort, not just with books on the subject, but actually with our children. After all, they have as much expertise as anyone about what is really going on. They can tell you their stories from social media chats or the latest apps that are trending, and how these are making them and other people feel and act. By learning alongside our children, we can be a much more effective advisor to them. Especially when they really need us.

Playing alongside our children

There are some books that somewhat radically propose that adults should encourage their children to play and interact online as much as they want to. They say that parents should not fear games like *Fortnite* that seem to grab children's attention, because they are the modern-day educators of vital social and emotional skills. They are the new playgrounds where children learn how to live. I understand this argument, and I think it has some merits. There is no reason why children can't learn important values and social skills in an online game. They might learn about following the rules, building alliances based on trust with other players, how to mediate conflict and how to communicate well with other players. In this sense, the cyber-playgrounds are similar to the school playgrounds where children also learn through the good and not-so-good actions of others.

However, there are some key differences between the cyber and school playgrounds our children live in. The first is the content of the games. Some of the more popular games are actually based on violence. The key to winning is to kill all of the enemies. This is hardly, I would say, conducive to developing the values of compassion and kindness. The second difference is that many children play games on their own and sometimes behind closed doors.

Popular games, like FIFA and Mario Kart, were traditionally played by friends or siblings in the same room. Today, children are increasingly playing games alone, wearing headsets, and their interactions are mediated through digital technologies. Even if they are playing them in the front room, it is hard for us to know what is going on. We can see when children are upset or hurt in real life, but we can't see if they are making other children, perhaps on the other side of the world, upset and hurt.

We must provide a safety net for our children in case they are feeling upset or hurt by their online interaction. But we also must challenge them when we think it is necessary and ask them difficult questions about their online interactions and if they might be hurting others. We can do this in our role as advisors and we can do this more successfully if we try to play alongside our children. This means taking the controller and asking them to teach us how to play the game. By playing the game, we learn how it affects us and how it might be affecting our children. This requires us to be present.

The moments we are present become a golden opportunity for our children to explain to us how games work and what the challenges and issues associated with playing them are. They also offer a chance for us to talk about character and cyber-wisdom as we play together. After all, many games are about stories, and stories, as I'll show you in the last part of this book, can be a great basis for character education.

CHAPTER 9: KEY MESSAGES

- We cannot teach our children to thrive online; we must help them learn how to do this themselves. This calls for us to act as advisors, playing the role of coach, mentor, supporter and facilitator of learning.

- Children develop their character and cyber-wisdom when they reflect on their experiences of living in the cyber-world. This is called experiential learning.

- We can't be snowplough or helicopter educators – children often learn more when they make mistakes. Our job is to offer advice and support to come back from and learn from these mistakes.

- We have to try to build partnerships with our children, tackling the ups and downs of living in the cyber-world together. At the heart of good partnerships are good conversations.

- It is important to seek out opportunities to learn with and alongside our children in the cyber-world – the best advisors are those who know their subject. To be voluntary digital immigrants we must play online alongside our children.

10

Be a Character Champion

'Character does count. For too long we have gotten by in a
society that says the only thing right is to get by and the
only thing wrong is to get caught. Character is doing
what's right when nobody is looking.'
J. C. Watts[1]

Julius Caesar Watts rose to fame as an American football star before switching to politics. Given his name, he was perhaps destined to be famous. As a sports star and politician, Julius no doubt knew a lot about character. The quotation above turned out to be prescient. If there is ever a place where our characters are at their most public when no one is looking, it is when we interact with others online. When we post something publicly on social media, rarely is anyone looking over our shoulders, but anyone, anywhere, might see it. What we post says a great deal about our character. This is what this chapter is about. How we can be a champion for our children's characters to ensure they *do the right thing* when nobody is looking.

Being a character champion should come naturally to most parents. After all, who would not want their children to grow up with desirable qualities such as being courageous, resilient, compassionate and honest?

Our role is to help our children, as they grow up, to develop these qualities. This is, of course, much easier said than done. It is also not a linear task. It is likely to get messy at times. However, the rewards, if we are successful, are great. If our children develop the qualities of character that are conducive to flourishing, we can be more confident that they will live happy and successful lives – both online and offline.

It is for this reason that I believe that developing the character of my children is my primary role as a parent. Nothing, for me, is more important.

In this chapter I explain what a character champion looks like in practice and why we should strive to be one. In the final part of this book I tackle how we might cultivate character and cyber-wisdom in our children. In Part Four I also suggest resources, activities and strategies for this purpose.

Bringing an age-old understanding of character into the modern age

In the introduction to this book I explained how virtue ethics, or an ethical approach to living well that prioritises character, has recently been viewed as a viable alternative to utilitarianism (weighing up moral consequences) and deontology (creating moral rules) theories. In short, we need character if society and individuals are to flourish.

Virtue ethics is both the oldest and the newest kid on the block. Virtue ethics is the oldest of the three most prominent moral theories; it just went out of fashion for a while. The ancient roots of virtue ethics lie in the writings of Plato, but are more significantly found in the philosophy of Aristotle. Aristotle, the Greek philosopher, lived between 384 and 322 BC. So how could his musings back then have any relevance for the digital world today? The answer is in the core tenets of his virtue theory that he outlined in one of his most famous books, *Nicomachean Ethics*. Although these tenets all need modernising, they provide the foundations for a theoretical approach that is hard to argue with and has stood the test of time. The three central concepts that, as character champions, we must keep in mind are: *eudaimonia* (commonly translated as happiness or flourishing), *arête* (commonly translated as excellence or virtue) and *phronesis* (commonly translated as practical or moral wisdom).

The reason that virtue ethics is somewhat back in favour is a reaction to the failures of deontological or rules-based ethics. As I have said previously, making rules and ascribing duties to people is nigh-on impossible in the online world. Instead, we can see how virtue ethics is nicely attuned to helping us understand the reciprocal relationships between technological structures and human agencies. Rules, in many ways, are too rigid for the fast-moving pace of digital technology. They are not fleet-footed enough to deal with the ever-changing nature of technology – we need to write rules now for technologies that don't exist. Virtue ethics is not so reliant on predicting the future, as it relies on one's conduct in the moment. It does not require laws or people to enforce them. It relies on us self-policing ourselves. Writing the *right* thing on a social networking site is not simply a matter of following the rules, or assessing likely consequences; it involves making wise, virtuous decisions about what we do and do not post.

I have only scratched the surface of the main components of Aristotelian virtue-ethical philosophy. Up until now I have made reference to the concepts and ideas that are most useful for the arguments that I am making in this book. Much greater detail on the ideas of Aristotle and those who followed in his footsteps have been provided by my academic colleagues.[2] My focus here is on the practice of these concepts in real life, in the here and now. When theory meets practice is when things can get more complex. Theory, when written down, can look pure and perfect. It often makes sense when we read it and try, in a hypothetical sense, to apply it to our lives. However, the world is not neat and we can't simply 'apply' theory and assume certain outcomes will be realised. If only it were so.

We humans live complex lives in complex societies. Therefore, applying the theory of character will take some trial and error. Aristotle himself was a naturalist. This means he did not believe in pure theory alone, but believed that theory should be shaped by the realities of the world. Well, this is what we need to do as parents; to become Aristotle's experimenters trying out his theories and reshaping them to fit in today's world. This is what this chapter is about – how we might go about applying a theory of character to inform how we live our lives.

Addressing the common challenges of character

Before showing how the concepts of flourishing, virtue and wisdom guide our roles as character champions, it is important to address some of the well-known challenges to character-based moral theory that prioritises wisdom and virtue. These are outlined below and for each of the challenges I provide a defence.

Challenge one: Sounds good in theory, but virtue ethics does not tell us what to do in practice

One of the most common criticisms is that virtue ethics does not provide an adequate guide to what action should be undertaken in specific circumstances. The charge goes that although virtue ethics sounds like a useful theory, it falls down in practice; that in today's world, to keep order, we need clearly defined rules, together with consequences if we don't adhere to them. On such a reading, virtue ethics is idealistic, as it does not give us clear guidance for behaviour.

The esteemed philosopher Julia Annas gives us some excellent tools with which to challenge this assumption. She turns the tables on the deontologists by stating that virtue ethics does give us rules and provide guidance for living morally, both generally and also in any given situation.[3] Annas believes there are such things as 'virtue rules' and that they provide guidance on what to do in most situations. We can see being compassionate or acting honestly as virtue rules. What is the virtue rule when we witness unkindness online? It's to be courageous. It is to try to tackle those who are being unkind and to be compassionate by reaching out to the person who has been hurt. The skill is knowing when and how much to apply each virtue in each situation.

These are 'skills' that Annas claims we can learn. They are human qualities that we can hone over time – we can get better or more skilful at enacting them. Annas says it is a bit like learning to play an instrument. This, of course, involves hard work, both by those learning the virtue rules and by parents and teachers tasked with teaching them.

We can help our children to learn about virtue rules by:

- Helping them understand that human qualities such as compassion, honesty, courage and integrity can be viewed as virtue rules. There are times when they are expected to show these qualities. We can do this by talking to our children about the importance of these and other virtues.

- Helping them learn how to hone these virtue rules. This means learning when is the right time to display the virtue and also in what amount. We can do this by helping our children reflect on the different times they have displayed one or more virtues and judge what went well and what they might do differently next time. To frame the discussion in the positive, you might use phrases like *what went well?* and *what would be even better?* as conversation starters.

Challenge two: We change our characters to suit different situations

A well-known critique of virtue ethics comes from a group that have been called the 'situationists'. Their central charge is that character virtues are not stable; moral responses are dependent on particular situations.[4] For example, we do not consistently act with compassion or honesty on social media and might also act cruelly or dishonestly depending on the situation.

Further, researchers who have adopted this view claim they have data to prove it.[5] The situationists use this data to construct arguments that disagree with Aristotle's belief that character traits are firm and unchangeable, and suggest instead that there are forces that come into play, which are dependent on the particularities of the moral dilemma. They point to evidence that shows that we make up our minds about how to act, depending on the circumstances of any given situation. On the face of it, this appears to contradict any belief that our character develops over time through acquiring virtuous habits.

Although this line of argument seems persuasive, it misunderstands virtue-ethical theory. Most virtue ethicists understand that few, if any, people are genuinely virtuous all the time. This is the normative ideal, a goal to strive for, but one that is not always attainable. The defenders of virtue ethics state that when we make poor moral decisions, it is because we have not applied practical wisdom correctly. Practical wisdom, as we will see, is eminently situational. This is one of the arguments for character education that focuses on honing practical wisdom. We need education that provides a scaffolding for learning when we don't get things right or our actions do not have virtuous outcomes. The strategies outlined in the last chapter of this book are designed to help children make more right decisions more often; however, there are no guarantees they always will. Very few, if any of us, always make the wisest moral decision. The key is that we are striving for this goal.

We can help our children learn that character virtues are not situational by:

- talking to them about the human qualities we think are the most important and how we try to display them in various situations – even in those when it is hard to do so;

- explaining that the display of character normally involves some thinking and not just jumping in. Most of us have to think and decide what is the right combination of virtues to show in any given situation.

Challenge three: We know what to do but we don't do it

A third challenge comes from within the virtue-ethics ranks and has been described as one of the profoundest problems. Described by some as the moral gap, it was most recently identified by the psychologist Augusto Blasi.[6] In order to understand this problem, we need to know a little about the work of Lawrence Kohlberg, a Harvard psychology professor. Kohlberg developed a model that, he argued, showed the stages that young people develop ethically. Inspired by Piaget's work, he claimed there are six stages of moral development, and these can be seen in three levels, moving from the pre-conventional, to the conventional, to the post-conventional. As we develop, according to the theory, we move from obedience to an understanding of universal principles that we aspire to adhere to. The model was extremely popular and is still used by some today. It has been largely rejected, partly because of its methodology, which equated an individual's moral maturity with the ability to offer solutions to far-fetched dilemmas, and partly by its ambition of supposing that students would act morally as a simple consequence of knowing how to act morally, or even of just knowing how to articulate convincing moral judgements.

This is where the work of Augusto Blasi comes in, and, in particular, his much-cited meta-analysis of empirical studies that gauged the relation between moral reasoning and moral behaviour. What Blasi found was that moral judgement plays, at best, a modest role in motivating moral action. In his experiments, Blasi discovered that what young people said they would do when faced with one of the Kohlberg ethical dilemmas is not what they would actually do in practice. I have also found this in my research. Young people, when faced with a hypothetical dilemma, often give an answer that is closer to the most virtuous course of action. When I ask them afterwards if they would, in real life, actually carry out this action when online, several give reasons why they wouldn't. This is a moral gap: knowing the good but not always doing the good. This challenge is persistent today and although many people are looking at educational approaches that might bridge the gap, few have been universally endorsed.

Although this 'gap' does present a problem for educators who are seeking strategies that will make it more likely that children will do the right thing when online, it does not mean we should do nothing.

It is clear that we can't teach practical wisdom in a didactic manner. It is also clear we can't make children act virtuously simply through a series of lessons. However, there are things we can do, including:

- showing our children we prioritise character and virtue in our daily lives even when it is hard to do so;

- providing our children with a language of character and virtues;

- using learning activities to prime or pre-arm our children to be better able to deal with online moral issues (some are suggested in Part Four);

- trying our best to exemplify cyber-wisdom and cyber-virtues in our everyday online lives;

- supporting and advising our children every day as they live their lives in their cyber-worlds.

I expand more on these approaches throughout the book. None of them are going to do any harm and they should all do some good. Most importantly, they all require that we act as character champions.

Challenge four: Why not just virtue ethics?

I have drawn out virtue ethics as the theory for the cyber-age for good reasons. However, by doing so, I don't want to underplay the importance of the alternative moral theories of deontology and utilitarianism. My argument is that, although these are useful, they are insufficient. To state otherwise would be overly reductionist for the following reason. In our lives we do not make distinctions between these theories when we are deciding on a course of action. Rarely would we stop and think about whether we are showing character, adhering to the rules or thinking about possible consequences when we, for example, keep to the speed limit while driving through a crowded town. We are probably unconsciously thinking about all three. We are constantly drawing on a number of considerations when making decisions about what action should be taken in any given situation. This is because ethics is complex and our lives are complex.

Drawing lines of comparison between the theories is a useful intellectual exercise, as it helps tease out what strategies are available. But we also need to put them back together and get on with our lives.

What is required is a non-reductionist approach to moral philosophy and a greater recognition about the complexity of life. I believe pluralistic models that integrate, in a non-reductionist way, strong notions of duty, consequence and virtue are preferable to taking any single one on its own at face value. Life, including our lives online, is not trivial or simplistic, and we should use all tools at our disposal to help make meaning of it. It is for this reason that rules and consequences are featured in the more practical sections of this book and are also built into the THRIVE and REACT models.

Although virtue ethics is not without its critics or challenges, it is the contention of this book that it provides useful guidance for online morality. It is flexible and embraces a wider range of possibilities than rule-based or outcome-based theories. Virtue ethics has much to offer those of us seeking ways to educate children to live a good digital life. For a virtue ethicist, the answer to the question 'How should I behave online?' is 'Virtuously and through displays of cyber-wisdom.' A virtue-ethical educational approach puts an emphasis on cultivating attitudes and dispositions that enable people to do the right thing when rules are absent, and the consequences are not obvious.

Why be a character champion?

One of the fiercest debates in the character-education world concerns the concept of indoctrination. In America a fear of indoctrination nearly killed off the character-education movement. It is a tricky debate but a pertinent one.

Do we want our children to always do what we tell them? Or do we want them to make their own decisions about the actions they take? If the latter, what should we do if these actions are not moral in our eyes? Who gets to say what is and what is not moral, particularly when there are no hard-and-fast rules? The big question is, how can we educate our children to do what we think is the right thing, without telling them they *must* do the right thing?

Critics who believe that character education is indoctrination by another name have a case to make. If character education is simply a didactic, one-way process based on predetermined outcomes, then this might be seen as indoctrinating character. For example, if a country was to tell its citizens that they must always be honest, specify exactly what honesty looked like, and punished people who were dishonest, many of us would think this was not right. Likewise, if we are to tell our children that they must be compassionate, define exactly what compassion looks like and punish them when they are not compassionate, this also feel like indoctrination. I would say that both these examples are not character education; instead, they are a form of behaviourism. They are detailing expected behaviour and the punishments for not adhering to them.

What is missing is children's voice and agency in the decision making. What is also missing is context – not all character-based decisions can be predetermined by a 'higher' force. Character education should not be about fixing the kids or simply telling them what to do or how to behave. Character education is an educational process that helps children to develop virtues through their own exploration of the world, self-discovery and learning. Our role is to help ensure that our children follow this path of discovery, to step in when the going gets hard, and to provide some language, tools and experience that help them navigate through it. Our role is not to take the lead at all times; instead, it is to sometimes take the lead, sometimes walk alongside our children and sometimes encourage them from a distance. This is not indoctrination; it is about being a character champion for them.

In this book I call for us to be character champions, not character enforcers. A champion is someone who supports an idea or goal, not someone who imposes one. As a character champion, our role is to (co-) establish some expectations and goals. It is to have high expectations about our children's character and it is to do what we can to help them become the best person they can be. But we must allow our children to become this person in their own way. They must be free to experiment and make mistakes.

The approach I outline might be best viewed as a difference between education and indoctrination. The best education, for me, teaches people how to learn for themselves. It is values-based and sets standards and expectations, as well as putting up some boundaries, but it does not offer a single set of irrefutable rules. Education is a process of looking for facts, finding different facts that might counter them and then making an informed decision. It is about being critical and analytical. Indoctrination is about influencing people to make them believe in a single set of facts, a single point of view, about a single way of life. One is about top-down enforcement and the other is about shared learning.

In the cyber-worlds we live in, I don't think we can be indoctrinating even if we want to be. I don't know the exact context of the cyber-world my daughter and son live in. It is always changing as new technology and apps are being invented. I can't impose some top-down, predetermined exact character 'rules', such as always be compassionate or kind online. My children are best placed to know what being compassionate or kind online looks like in their daily online lives and in each situation that demands these qualities. I can guide them and ask questions that help them to think about their actions and behaviour, but they make the decision about what they do. They must ultimately be in charge of sculpting the finer details of their own characters.

Being a character champion

If building character was like teaching maths, life as a parent or teacher would be pretty easy. We would have to put in the time and effort, but we would have a curriculum to follow. We would know what to do and when. We could set goals and targets and we could measure progress against these. Unfortunately, cultivating character is not like learning how to do calculations.

Character virtues are not facts. Let's take the example of courage, a virtue that is particularly important in the cyber-world where we want our children to explore but be aware of the risks of doing so. We can teach our children to know what courage means and give them examples of courage in action. We can do this simply by giving them a good dictionary and explaining times when we did or did not show courage and what the consequences were. We can also help our children see why courage is a good virtue to possess. You could show your children a film about a courageous person, then talk about the film with them after it finishes. We could also make this learning a bit more complex. For example, we could explain the idea that every virtue has a 'sweet spot'. In the case of courage, too much might be seen as rash and overconfident and not enough might be seen as cowardly.[7]

These activities will all help our children learn about the virtue of courage, but they won't necessarily make them more courageous. This can only happen when the rubber hits the road. When our children start to practise the virtue of courage. This is when we stop becoming a teacher and need to become a character champion. Here we need to be an exemplar and advisor as explained in the previous chapters, but what we should always be looking for is a way to make our children's character develop authentically.

This is where it gets hard. To be authentically courageous they have to want to show courage (be motivated), see themselves as courageous (see the quality as part of their identity) and be able to notice situations that stand in need of them being courageous (have perception). Then it gets even harder. They need to know when to show the right amount of courage, in the right situation at the right time; they need to have superb judgement or wisdom. Not just once, but in every situation they face online and offline. Finally, it gets even harder still, as it might be that to be courageous, they have to be disloyal to a friend. For example, if they decide to tell their teacher about mean comments that one of their friends has been posting on WhatsApp. The virtues of courage and loyalty clash. Should they still be courageous in these situations? Although we can see what qualities our children need to develop, we can't teach virtue motivation, identity, perception and wisdom.

Many people believe that character is developed over time and with hard work until good actions become habits. The following well-known saying has been attributed to several people, but most prominently to the Chinese philosopher Lao Tzu, who was credited with founding the philosophical system of Taoism:

Watch your thoughts, they become your words;
watch your words, they become your actions;
watch your actions, they become your habits;
watch your habits, they become your character;
watch your character, it becomes your destiny.

Aristotle would have agreed with the sentiment of that quote. He believed that character virtues are developed through habit and that there is thus a requirement for individuals to practise them constantly. He said, 'We become just by performing just acts, temperate by performing temperate ones, brave by performing brave ones.'[8]

How to be a character champion

In the bullet points below, I explain how you might become more of a mindful champion of character:

- Help your children understand that you think their character matters. Tell them it is one of the most important things you look for in them.

- Be a cheerleader for your children's character. Point out and praise them when they make wise, virtuous decisions – especially ones that are hard to make.

- Talk to your children about character all the time. Help them develop a language they can use to reflect on their own characters and how they display different qualities in online situations.

- When watching TV and films or reading books with your children, point out and discuss the character qualities displayed by different characters. Use these as examples and, where appropriate, exemplars.

- Be understanding. When they display the wrong virtue or no virtue in a particular situation, you should always discuss this with them but not necessarily punish them for it.

- Be patient and try to understand their side of the story when things go wrong. Ask them for their reasons when they have undertaken an action that shows the best or not-so-good sides of their character.

- Run some of the activities in this book with your children. These will help you be more explicit in your role as a character champion.

What it means to THRIVE

The overarching message of this book is that if we can help our children develop character and cyber-wisdom, they are more likely to thrive online, which is the T of the REACT model. Part Three covers the individual components of the THRIVE model, but I want to close Part Two by explaining what it means to thrive.

To thrive online is to live well in a cyber-world worth living in.

Aristotle thought that the supreme good for human beings is being in the state of *eudaimonia*, to be in a state of flourishing. Thriving is a common synonym for flourishing. The state of flourishing or thriving should be both complete and self-sufficient. It cannot be bettered. Thriving should therefore be the goal for all of us.

But what sort of thriving am I talking about? One way to think about the different ways we define thriving is to consider a common synonym for the term: happiness. There are two ways we could see happiness. One is gained from sensual pleasure or what some might call hedonistic happiness; the other we gain from the practice of the virtues. One type of happiness is more fleeting, more temporary and linked to particular sensory-enthused situations. The other type of happiness, the one I think really matters, is more about a long-lasting commitment to a particular purpose or meaningful relationships. Thriving online should be less about the former and more about the latter.

It is not about gaining short-term pleasure, from, say, beating a friend in an online game, or watching a good film online (although there is nothing wrong with these and many other pursuits we gain pleasure from). Thriving online is something more enduring, but takes more work over a lifetime. It is a place that we constantly need to strive for and that we may, on occasions, lose our way to. It comes not from seeking individual gratification, but from thinking about how our actions affect ourselves and others over the longer term.

A way to see this clearly is to consider the different type of friendships our children might make online. Aristotle believed there to be three main types of friendship. The first two, for pleasure and utility, might be enjoyable, but they are incomplete as they are only valuable because of what we gain from them. These types of friendship are based on gaining reward for oneself. The third type might be called character friendships. These are long-term, mutually reciprocal friendships that are not based on extrinsic rewards. They are the types of friendship that involve give-and-take and looking out for others. Sometimes social media can make us overly obsessed with ourselves. It makes us seek out instant and hopefully positive feedback and affirmation. A character friendship is not about using social media for the good of oneself but about employing it for the good of others. A cyber-world that is a flourishing world will contain more character friendships and fewer of those that are simply based on reward or utility.

After all, we can only truly thrive if those we share our worlds with are also thriving.

CHAPTER 10: KEY MESSAGES

- Our character is what we do when no one is watching. Character is therefore especially important in the cyber-age.

- Our role as character champions is to help our children to perform more right than wrong actions online when they are on their own.

- Character is the central concept in the moral theory of virtue ethics. Virtue ethics differs from deontological moral theory – which prioritises rules – and utilitarianism – which prioritises the consequences of actions.

- Being a character champion does not mean indoctrinating our children to be a particular sort of person. It is not overly moralistic. It is about having a clear focus on character with our children and helping them come to see why character and cyber-wisdom are important qualities to develop.

- The ultimate aim is that we help children make the right decision about their online actions more often than not. In time, virtuous actions will hopefully become virtuous habits.

Summary of Part Two:
The Journey to Thriving Online

Part Two of the book describes the journey through the REACT model in the following way:

R (ground rules): We start by developing rules, or what might be better called *ground rules*. Ground rules are the foundations that character is built upon. They are necessary but insufficient on their own. The ground rules will be initiated and put in place by us, but should be co-constructed with our children. They provide a set of minimum expectations as well as the rules for engagement with cyber-technologies.

E (exemplars): The first step to reducing or ultimately removing the rules is taken by showing our children how to use cyber-technologies wisely. We do this by being an *exemplar*. Good character is largely caught by children. They are most likely to catch it from those around them. What we do matters, as it shapes what our children do. We must model the character and wisdom that we hope our children will develop.

A (advisors): Once we have created an environment that will make it more likely our children can thrive online, we have to allow them greater freedom to experiment themselves. Here we must adopt the role of an *advisor*. An advisor is a form of teacher, but one that is a co-constructor and partner in learning rather than a sage on the stage. We become less of the rule-maker, and more of a coach, mentor and supporter. In these roles we are on hand to help our children deal with the issues and challenges they face in their cyber-worlds, not just tell them about what we know and think. Our children, in their experimentation, might not get everything right. We must adopt strategies that help them learn from their online actions.

C (character champions): Ground rules, exemplars, authentic experience and advice contribute to building *character* and honing cyber-wisdom. Developing these qualities in our children should be the goal for all of us. This is all about us reminding our children every day about the importance of character. It is about us initiating conversations with our children about character and asking them when they feel their character has been tested online. It is also about letting go and trusting them to do the right thing and make wise decisions. We know we have succeeded when our children make autonomous, critical judgements and choose the right character quality to show at the right time.

T (thrive): If we are able to successfully make and enforce ground rules, be an exemplar, be an advisor and be a character champion, we will help our children *thrive online*. This part of the model reminds us to focus our intentions on building the six qualities that comprise the THRIVE model (covered in Part Three). As they grow up in the cyber-world, we must help our children to be thoughtful, to be human, to reason well, to show integrity, to be virtuous and to be an exemplar to others. If they show these qualities, they will be more likely to thrive online. It will also be more likely that those they interact with online will thrive.

Part Three

THRIVE

11
Be Thoughtful

To be thoughtful is the first component of the THRIVE model. It is one of the most important qualities our children need to possess if they are to thrive online and ensure those around them are also thriving.

There are two parts to being thoughtful and both are vital for our children to develop:

1.   To be thoughtful is to be kind, compassionate, understanding and caring.

2.   To be thoughtFULL is to be reflective and to think before we act.

We need our children to aim their focus differently for each type:

1.   To be thoughtful is to think about others first.

2.   To be thoughtFULL is to think about what they themselves are doing first.

I will now explain more about each of these two types.

Thoughtful – to be caring in the cyber-world

At its best, to be thoughtful is to think and act in a caring way towards others. In the cyber-world this might take a number of forms, including;

•   reaching out to someone you have not heard from for a while to check they are okay;

- staying in touch with a friend who has moved away;

- joining a group that is campaigning for a positive cause;

- stepping into an argument on social media if you see someone is getting hurt;

- raising money for a good cause;

- staying in touch with an elderly relative over email or social media.

But the virtue of thoughtfulness also has a flipside. To be unthoughtful is to be uncaring and unthinking of others. In the cyber-world this might take a number of forms, including;

- bullying someone in your school online;

- deliberately trolling a famous person on Twitter;

- not doing anything when you witness a friend being bullied;

- sharing images or making comments that you know will embarrass the original author;

- posting an anonymous comment that you know will hurt people;

- not replying to a message on social media when you know the recipient will be hurt if you don't.

The Internet provides our children with ample opportunities to be caring or uncaring. If the cyber-world is going to be a pleasant place to live, we need to encourage thoughtfulness in our children – we must help them to understand why thinking about and caring for others is important. Even when it takes great courage and strength to do so.

Technology as the driver for thoughtfulness

The good news is that cyber-technologies offer our children the opportunity to care about more people more often. They can also use the Internet to search for places that they could direct their care and compassion towards. The Internet can expose our children to injustices around the world, causes and issues that they might not know about otherwise. The technologies not only open our children's eyes to issues that demand care, but also provide a tool that our children can use to do something about them. The technology allows them to reach out to people in diverse places – all in an instant.

There is a whole new language growing up around the idea of helping others online. We now talk about those people who use the Internet to make a difference as 'cyber-citizens' or 'digital citizens'. The Internet has become the easiest and most convenient way for children and young people to reach out to others and try to help them. It has made it possible for our children to show a social conscience and reach out to people without leaving their homes. They can connect with big issues and concerns through social media and they can be active and feel part of something beyond themselves.

There are some good reasons why children might be particularly attracted to reaching out and helping others online. First, our children have grown up with the technologies, and using them is second nature for many. The technology engages them on their own terms. This makes it more likely that they will see their smartphone or tablet as a natural means to civic participation. The second, and perhaps more important, reason is that technologies massively increase our children's sense of self-efficacy. Civic and political power used to be largely the proviso of those who controlled the means of communication – normally the media and politicians. The Internet has changed all this. Anyone with a computer and Wi-Fi can now broadcast their ideas to the world. As an example, think of the grassroots movements on Twitter, which led to the Arab Spring. This uprising was started by young people using technology as the basis for increasing their efficacy and therefore their power. This movement led to regime change on a grand scale.

I'm not suggesting our children are involved in anything so dramatic – but the principle is the same. Technology can give people a voice, which they could use for the common good. Some children don't see the Internet simply as a tool for entertainment but as a means to fulfilling their sense of civic purpose. Because of the features of the Internet, children can join with many other people (most of whom they won't know) to undertake direct positive action on local, national or global concerns.

There is lots of evidence to suggest that young people in the UK and elsewhere are taking up this opportunity. For example, a report called *Service Generation* showed how social media had created new digital spaces, significant for those interested in undertaking meaningful and positive social action.[1] Interestingly, the specific kind of social action these users are interested in differs by gender, insofar as girls were more interested in volunteering, and boys in protest and activism. A subsequent report entitled *Generation X* found that 84 per cent of teachers thought that the new networks and forms of engagement provided by social media are – or can be – just as effective as traditional forms of engagement (such as joining a political party or voting).[2] The survey revealed that substantial numbers of young people use social media to become engaged with social issues: for example, 38 per cent of those surveyed stated they had signed a petition online; 29 per cent had used Facebook or Twitter to raise awareness of a cause; 21 per cent had 'liked' a political cause or group that they agreed with; and 19 per cent had donated money online. Teachers are also noting an increase in this type of engagement among their pupils. Over half of teachers reported that they had noticed teenagers using social media to become involved in politics and good causes.

Thoughtfulness takes more than just a click

Before we get carried away, it is important to sound a note of caution.

Important questions have to be asked about the form and content of online expressions of thoughtfulness. Are they all really thoughtful? Is clicking a 'like' button online the same quality of thoughtfulness as going next door to help a neighbour? The rather disparaging term 'clicktivism' is used as a way to critique 'lazy' expressions of social action; for example, clicking a button to join a campaign on, say, animal welfare without really thinking about or engaging with the issue.

The Internet has made it easy for our children to join thousands of causes and campaigns without much effort – this has been given the term 'slacktivism'. This could have a negative impact on civic participation, as the amount of time spent online detracts from the time available for young people to participate in potentially more meaningful offline civic activities. It could also lead to moral licensing – children feel that they have done a good deed by signing an online petition and therefore don't have to do something in the 'real' world. Also, it might be argued that we express our thoughts and care for others better in person than virtually. In the cyber-world, children might become detached from reality by not actually seeing the issues they are volunteering for or supporting. Seeing things first-hand can drive up empathy.

Micro-volunteering

We need to help our children to participate in meaningful online social action. The national #iwill campaign has, since 2012, been encouraging young people to undertake meaningful social action for the benefit of others.[3] The group recognised early on the importance of digital technologies to enable more young people to do more for others. They promote the idea of micro-volunteering, which means to participate by devoting small increments of time through technology.

Micro-volunteering is perceived to be a good way to overcome the barriers to volunteering that stop some children participating, as volunteers undertake a series of tasks that can be done anytime, anywhere and on your own terms. For example, the Help from Home website suggests volunteering opportunities that take under one minute (such as voting on your favourite design for a charity campaign) to under thirty minutes (writing a blog about epilepsy).[4] The website includes hundreds of micro-volunteering opportunities, all of which, it boasts, can be undertaken in your pyjamas. A supposed advantage is that micro-volunteering has the potential to engage a larger and wider range of young people. Volunteering in this way might also be attractive to children who are not so outgoing.

I believe that, on balance, the Internet has given our children an amazing tool to connect with people around the world and to show care, compassion, thoughtfulness and understanding towards others. Sometimes this probably will be shallow and undertaken without much thought. Other times, it could actually change the world.

ThoughtFULL: Reflecting on our actions in the digital world

ThoughtFULLness is less about thinking about others. It is more about thinking about ourselves and our actions. It is to be introspective, to be self-examining and self-analysing. The quality of personal critical reflection is at the heart of being thoughtFULL.

If we can encourage our children to critically reflect and evaluate their use of cyber-technologies, they are more likely to thrive online. This is because reflection is a key component of cyber-wisdom. We learn through thinking about what we have done in different situations and what we might do differently in the future. Our role is to act as advisors in this situation, asking the right questions that will encourage thoughtfulness in our children. However, our children have to do the hard work. And it is hard work.

Taking the time to stop, look inwards and, if required, ask difficult questions is not easy for any of us. Many people, myself included, prefer to put off this sort of thinking and bash on regardless. This is the easier and often less courageous way to live. Being truly thoughtFULL is likely to be painful and requires vulnerability. It requires all of us to go back to places when we were not at our best and think about why. It requires us to relive painful memories and re-experience painful feelings. Research shows that we relive emotional pain more than physical pain.[5] But it is these feelings that often motivate us to take a different course of action next time a similar situation occurs. We sometimes need to feel pain to make changes in our lives. It is the same for our children.

It is for this reason that being thoughtFULL or *full* of thoughts is at the heart of character development. I cover the importance of reflection for developing character and cyber-wisdom in more depth in the last part of this book. Here, I want to show how we should encourage our children to reflect in two different ways. They need to undertake long-term macro-reflections and shorter-term micro-reflections.

Macro-reflection: Seeing the bigger picture

Macro-reflections are undertaken on a large scale. They are about looking at the big picture. For our children this means looking into their past and trying to imagine their future. It involves combining the daily micro-interactions they experience online and trying to see these more as a whole. This process will help children ask important questions like: does the technology make them better or worse? How does it change their character, their virtues and the ways they are with people?

The eighteen-year-old singer Billie Eilish seems to have undertaken a form of macro-reflection when she recently decided to stop using social media. She said, 'The Internet is ruining my life so I turned it off.'[6] Another young pop star, Ed Sheeran, is also famous for getting rid of his phone for long periods of time.

Of course, macro-reflections are hard to carry out in practice. But this should not stop us helping our children to zoom out and try to look beyond their phone to a more distant horizon. They need to see how their history has been shaped since they were first given a smartphone or tablet. What does this journey look like? What were the parts of it they are proud of and when did they feel pain? What would they ultimately like to use their smartphone, computer or tablet for?

We can help our children carry out this sort of reflection in more or less formal ways. More formally, we could get them to sketch out on a piece of paper their relationship with technology since they first went online. This might take the form of a chart with a timeline on the x axis and highs and lows on the y axis. While doing this, they can talk through with you how they think it has shaped or even changed them at different times in their lives. At the end of this process they should have a better sense of their relationship with the Internet. This is a good basis to get our children to plan what they might do differently, how they might use the technology in better ways in the future. Less formal strategies would include a well-timed open question such as, 'How do you think your phone has changed you?', or, 'Can you imagine being in touch with your friends without the Internet?' Or, 'Can you imagine spending your evenings without the Internet?'

Micro-reflections: Pause before posting

The feature of cyber-technology that is perhaps the most addictive and damaging is that it allows for, and often seems to demand, instantaneous responses.

Instantaneous responses can be the killer of character.

Think about people who lose their reputations after one rash decision, for example an ill-conceived social media post. Unfortunately, we are sometimes judged by what we do once rather than what we do over the duration of a lifetime. This is one of the problems with living in the round-the-clock media age – everything is a story and often context is not taken into account. This is why we need to help our children develop the ability to carry out micro-reflections. To learn about the 'power of the pause'.

More and more people are understanding that we have to help our children make time to pause to think before they act online. For example, the BBC has recently launched a new app called 'Own It'.[7] The app encourages those who install it to think before they hit the send button. The app uses artificial intelligence to monitor how children are responding to posts they receive on social media. If the app detects that a response might not be appropriate, a message pops up. This message encourages the sender to think through their actions and to edit or delete the post before sending.

To make a wise decision on- or offline often requires time. Time to think, time to weigh up options, time to think about past similar experiences, time to check in with ourselves and what we think is important. This time is rarely afforded to us online; everything is sped up – the clue is in the name of popular apps like Instagram or Snapchat. These apps are popular as they allow, some might say demand, instant communication. Why is this different from having a conversation? Because online feedback loops that aid communication are not as effective. We can't see exactly how our instant messaging is affecting others; we are largely operating blind. What makes the situation worse is that what we write might never be deleted. There is a permanent black-and-white record of our words.

This is why micro-reflections should be encouraged. This is the power of the pause. The brief check-in before sending a message. If we can help our children re-read their messages and think about how they might be received, this might save them from sending poorly thought-through posts. The following approaches might be helpful ways to ensure your children pause before posting:

- Type the message, save it, and look at it another time.

- Deliberately leave your phone or tablet in another room for a while.

- Share the draft message with a friend to get their opinion.

- Turn off notifications so as not to be hounded for a response.

If our children learn to pause, they will have time to consider questions like:

- How will my message be received?

- Is there anything in my message that might cause offence?

- Would I be happy for someone to show me this message in five years' time?

- What does this message say about me?

- How were similar messages received last time?

- What evidence do I have that my message will be interpreted how I want it to be?

If our children can learn to pause before posting, they are more likely to be thoughtFULL. This means they must:

think about their actions in the past . . .
. . . be mindful in the present . . .
. . . and try to imagine their futures.

CHAPTER 11: KEY MESSAGES

- Being thoughtful is one of the most important qualities we can develop in our children to help them live well online.

- There are two parts to being thoughtful. Being thoughtful is about thinking of others and being thoughtFULL is about thinking through and reflecting on our actions.

- The Internet provides many excellent resources that help children be thoughtful – to be cyber-citizens and to reach out to help others online.

- Critical self-reflection is at the heart of being thoughtFULL.

- We must encourage our children to undertake macro-reflections – to look at the big picture and how the technology is making it more or less likely they will behave in virtuous ways.

- Instantaneous interactions can be the killer of character and therefore we also need our children to undertake micro-reflections. They should think before they participate in any online interaction, such as posting a potentially harmful message. We need them to learn about the power of the pause.

12

Be Human

Google Maps has made our lives easier, but has it made our lives better? Sometimes, when we are inconvenienced, we gain so much more from life – we just don't always realise it at the time.

To get lost in a strange city or rural village might be scary for some of us. But how often these days do we try to get over our fear by rolling down the window and speaking to a local to ask for directions? I don't. I avoid human interaction and regularly find myself looking down at my phone as I walk around a village or keeping my car windows up as Google Maps directs me around a city. The Internet has made our lives so much easier, but I am not sure it has made them richer. This is because it has the potential, if we are not careful, to make our lives less human. Stopping to ask someone directions is just one of the small but important human interactions that is being eroded by technology.

It took a few years for the World Wide Web to catch on after it was invented, with little fanfare, by Sir Tim Berners-Lee in 1989. It was not until around 1995 that commercial ventures such as Amazon, Hotmail and others really got going, and it was a good few years before giants such as Facebook would launch. The real gift that the Internet seemed to promise was that it enabled instantaneous, large-scale, global communication through bits and bytes. Digital data replaced, on a mass and global scale, much communication that had previously taken place face to face. MIT Professor Shirley Turkle dubbed this phenomenon 'alone together'.[1] The paradox that Turkle pointed out was that although cyber-technologies seemingly connect us more, they could actually lead us to greater solitude. Shirley Turkle's concern was that technology would lead to emotional and other breakdowns, as it creates a technological barrier stopping us from being fully human.

The science about how the Internet is changing us is complex and, as with much of the research into the Internet, it is not clear exactly what is happening. Some people have predicted a singularity – technology and humans amalgamating into one. Others argue it is having little effect on us. There are some studies that seem to be worth taking seriously, particularly those utilising the growing discipline of neuroscience. There is increasingly compelling evidence that the Internet is changing how our brains work. Research has shown how the Internet is reducing our attention spans, adversely affecting our memory and damaging real-life social interactions. Research by academics at four top universities, including Oxford and Harvard, found that time spent online could produce 'acute and sustained' alterations in the brain that could be harmful to children's development.[2] Interestingly, they found the opposite could be true in older adults experiencing cognitive decline, for whom the online environment may provide a source of positive cognitive stimulation. Although this, and other brain-related research, is in its infancy, research from such an esteemed group of researchers should not be ignored. At the very least, the research should make us all ask questions about how the Internet is affecting our humanity.

Despite rapid technology developments, I don't think we are heading towards a singularity in the near future. We need to keep our heads screwed on in this debate. We need to remember we are in control and that we choose how we integrate technology into society. This means constantly reminding ourselves (and our children) about what makes us human. We then need to ensure we preserve the bits we value about being human – this, I believe, is essential for our happiness and wellbeing.

IRL

Most of you will be familiar with acronyms used online such as LOL and YOLO. Not so long ago there was another popular acronym: IRL. It stood for *in real life*, and was used to signify that life online might be different to that offline. When I was interviewing young people around that time, I noticed that it was common for many of them to describe their online and offline worlds differently. They would use phrases like 'in the real world' to indicate that they felt the rules were different online.

This might be construed as simply semantics, but at the time I believed it was deeper. I found clues to why this might be the case in speaking to young people and asking them to describe the Internet. One thirteen-year-old boy explained to me that, 'The Internet gives you a break from real life; if the rules were the same then there isn't a point going online. There is more freedom on the Internet.' Since conducting this research only a few years ago, I think times have already moved on, and rather than young people seeing their online and offline worlds as different, today they operate between the two seamlessly. This might be a cause for concern for any parent who is worried about their children being tethered to their phones – and constantly sharing information and updating their status. Seeing their online lives as an extension of their offline lives can lead to the need for constant affirmation at any time and in any place. This might mean they stop being able to undertake 'autonomous self-reflection' and become overly reliant on feedback from others.

However, this increasingly seamless connection between offline and online lives has a flipside to it, one that might make the job of parenting easier. We can present a unified approach to character and character education. IRL is no different from online life. In both, children need to show up and show the best sides of themselves – driven by their feelings, emotions and hopefully a desire to act with virtue and wisdom.

Being better humans, not just having better technologies

In the remainder of this chapter I outline a number of areas that you could discuss with your children that will help them remember what it means to be human – especially when the technology is seemingly taking over.

1. Judge friendships qualitatively, not quantitatively

Don't let your children fall into the technology trap. The Internet largely runs on binary algorithms and, if we are not careful, we can all start to think this way too. For me, this is not a human way to live. The best things in life – love, friendships, experiences – should (if they have to) be measured qualitatively, not quantitatively. We have to describe them, not count them.

The rise of social media, and in particular Facebook and Instagram, somewhat challenges this premise. I know friends of my children who count their friends by the number they have and not by the quality of them. This is because these apps and others are driven by metrics – it is part of the business models of the companies who make money from them. When we log into the apps we are told how many friends, followers and likes we have. Do we count these or look at what each one of them individually means to us? It is our duty, I believe, to remind our children that friendships are messy, but they are also rich and they certainly should mean more than a number.

Numbers are fixed and static but friendships are changing – this is what makes them so compelling and wonderful. We grow closer and less close to people. We fall in and out of love. We have to interpret what other people are thinking and feeling about us. The more open we are, the more we know and learn about others. When we remember that friendships are rich, we are more likely to think about how we are treating other people; interacting and living with values. We see people around us as human and not simply as digits.

So, the next time your children tell you about the number of 'likes' they have, ask them to describe what moves them or makes them feel good about the individuals behind these 'likes'.

Encourage them to think about their friendships qualitatively rather than quantitatively.

2. Have a conversation about value versus values

Many of the early pioneers of the Internet had grand, socially driven aspirations for the technology. They saw it as a way that people could connect on a vast scale, across territories, to promote collaboration. It could be a force for good, as it would unite people to tackle global issues such as war, the environment and inequality. Their goals for the Internet were very much values-driven. Many of these early pioneers were disheartened when the dot-com revolution started, and the Internet became less about values and more about economic value. Success was measured not in terms of how people connected online, but of how much money these connections made for companies. Human traffic became the value, leading to terms such as clickbait. News stories about companies that had attracted more than a billion users and floated on the stock market for vast sums became increasingly prevalent. These news stories, I think, are more about monetary value than human values.

By helping our children to see the difference between online monetary value and values, we can help them see a path to cyber-wisdom. Are they using technologies in a way that adds value to the big companies or are they using them in a way that spreads positive human values? Do they see the Internet as a tool that furthers capitalism or compassion, growth or gratitude, income or integrity? The more we have this conversation with our children, the more we can help them see that their character matters and that, even though they might think they are insignificant, what they do online really matters.

This does not mean they should reject Big Tech and not use Instagram or Twitter; just that they should think about whether they are using these companies or the companies are using them.

Having a conversation about value versus values will encourage children to consider whether they are using the freedoms these apps offer to bring about the sorts of global, positive changes to humanity that many of the early Internet pioneers envisaged.

3. Put cyber-wisdom before artificial intelligence

The more sophisticated the technology gets, the harder we will have to try to remind ourselves, and our children, what it means to be human. Speculation that we are moving towards a technological singularity is now discussed openly in serious news and documentary programmes. Some think that the singularity will come about because technology is implanted into our brains; for others, because technology itself develops super-intelligence that is beyond that of humans. There are academics working in university departments dedicating their lives to researching the topic. Most commentators believe that the time when technology develops super-intelligence will be well beyond any of our lifetimes, but it is one that is increasingly possible to imagine.

Driving the march towards singularity is artificial intelligence (AI). AI is a term that gets bandied around without much thought. It is generally taken to mean the ability of machines to perform tasks digitally and therefore replace human beings. AI innovators are seeking to endow technology with the intellectual characteristics of humans, such as the ability to reason and learn from the past. They are starting to be successful. AI is replacing humans in many spheres. It began by replacing those in traditional blue-collar jobs such as manufacturing and now there are serious books about technology replacing white-collar jobs such as teaching, law, accounting and many more.[3]

In his most recent book *Globotics*, Richard Baldwin, a professor of international economics, explains that we need to know what AI and robots are not very good at to understand where humans are most needed in the workplace.[4] If we believe that one of the roles of education is to ensure we have the qualities to get jobs, then we need to start thinking about whether we are educating children with qualities that AI and robots don't have. Baldwin tells us that machines are not very successful at acquiring social intelligence, emotional intelligence, creativity, innovation skills or the ability to deal with unknown situations. These are qualities that make us human, qualities that education must seek to develop. They are the qualities parents and teachers need to focus on cultivating, for jobs will be available in these 'sheltered sectors', shielded from automation. In the language of this book, they are character qualities: they require resilience, tolerance, compassion, empathy, courage and a whole host of other virtues. More than anything else, they also require (cyber-)wisdom to coordinate these virtues. Such human qualities are the basis of real interpersonal relationships.

The boss of Google, Sundar Pichai, thinks that AI has many positives for humans – he boldly stated in a recent presentation that it will do more for humanity than fire. In the same speech he stressed that AI had to ultimately be accountable to people.[5] If the next generation grow up understanding the importance of character and cyber-wisdom, it is more likely that future technologies will be designed with humans in mind and in charge.

The question we need our children to think about is this: does AI mean we can stop thinking, and more importantly, that we can stop feeling? We should ask our children these questions, as they will be living with the consequences of the AI revolution.

4. Pick up the phone

I bought my daughter a mobile phone package with 500 minutes of free calls a month. Guess how many of these minutes she normally uses? Almost none. Times have changed. It was not that long ago that a classic caricature was of a teenager hogging the phone while their irate parents tried to get them to hang up.

I think we should now be saying, 'Pick up the phone.'

There is nothing inherently wrong with text communication, I just feel it is an inferior form of communication and at times not very human – think of the stories we hear about people who have broken up with their partners by text. But there are less important situations where the human connection gained through a phone call is also important. We need to help our children develop cyber-wisdom so they know when to pick up the phone (or meet people) to deal with sensitive, troubling or challenging situations in a more human way.

Activity

To remind our children what it means to be human in a technological age, I suggest framing conversations with them around these two ideas:

- **Dualism – the division of something into two opposing and contrasting ideas.** In our conversation we need children to reject dualist accounts of technology. To reject dualism is to remind our children that not all technological developments are necessarily good or bad. You might ask your children what they think are the best and worst things about the Internet and why?

- **Determinism – events that happen external to our will.** In the conversation, we want to help children to reject determinism. We need to remind them that they are the users of technology, and what they do with it matters. You might ask your children if they feel in control of their technologies, such as their smartphone, or do they feel it controls them? What could they do to take back more control?

To think and talk about dualism and determinism is to think and talk about humanity. It is to remind our children that they have agency. They can be critical. They can be reflective. They have freedom to choose what technologies and apps they use and what they use them for.

CHAPTER 12: KEY MESSAGES

- Technology has brought humans many benefits, but it has also taken away some good things about being human. We need to help children think about how cyber-technologies have affected their sense of what it means to be human.

- We should help our children 'measure' their friendships online qualitatively, not quantitatively – to evaluate how their friends contribute positively to their lives, rather than just count the number of likes, followers or friends they have.

- It is good to have a values-or-value conversation with your children. Ask them how they can turn the tables on Big Tech – rather than being used to raise share prices and value, how can they use the technology to share and spread common values.

- AI might take away some of the more mundane jobs, but it can't, as yet, undertake important human roles that require feelings, emotions and other human qualities. Remind your children that these qualities are what mark them out from technology now and in the future.

- We should encourage children to pick up the phone more, to have sensitive and important conversations in a more human way.

- Whereas AI makes decisions based on calculations using data from the past, cyber-wisdom is about decisions made in specific moments, in specific contexts and in the present. Cyber-wisdom is the human quality that is vital for everyday living with others.

13
Be ReasonABLE

The term 'reasonable' is defined in dictionaries using the following words: good sense, good judgement, fair, practical, not extreme or excessive.

These are some of the same ingredients required for the possession of practical wisdom. To be reasonable online is to try to show practical or cyber-wisdom. It is to demonstrate good judgement when faced with a dilemma. In our children's online worlds these relate to moral issues including sexting, plagiarism, bullying, misinformation and others.

Being reasonable in this sense is not a passive quality. It is also not a quality easily possessed. It takes time to develop, and conviction to show. It is about thinking and then trying to take the most ethical course of action in any given situation. It is ultimately about doing.

Carrie James and others have conducted research that shows that many immoral activities carried out by children and young people are not undertaken on purpose.[1] James calls these 'ethical blind spots' and says they occur because young people can easily become disconnected from the 'real world'. This is because they are not sensitive enough to moral concerns found in their online worlds. They have not learnt how to tune in to them properly. James says we need to develop what she calls *conscientious connectivity* in our children.

This might also be called being 'reasonABLE'.

To be reasonABLE is to think through online actions before taking them. To be able to spot a dilemma, weigh up competing courses of action and choose the best one to take.

There is no easy way to teach our children to be reasonABLE, though there are some strategies described in the last part of this book.

There are, however, three main steps towards being reasonABLE that we can help our children to take.

- Step one is for children to notice issues online that call for a character-based response. They have to develop perception and foresight.

- Step two is to notice that they have different courses of action open to them – to be able to identify and weigh up alternative options. This requires them to think through the alternative ways they could respond and try to choose the best one.

- Step three is to actually carry out the choice that is deemed to be the best course of action.

To be reasonABLE is about applied cognition. It is to think and do. After doing, it is about thinking again – to ask questions such as, 'What did we learn and what might we do differently next time?' Through this ongoing process the ability to be reasonABLE is strengthened.

Why do we need our children to be reasonABLE?

To be reasonABLE is to develop a quality that the ancient Greeks and, in particular, the philosopher Aristotle thought was important. As I have mentioned previously, he called it *phronesis*. Translations of *phronesis* have included practical reasoning, practical wisdom, good sense, moral discernment, moral insight and prudence. It is about reasoning not just for the good of oneself but for the good of others. It is a pro-social quality.

To be reasonABLE is to have a finely honed sense of moral judgement and one that can be directed to any situation. It is to be able to:

do the right thing
at the right time

with the right people
in the right situation
in the right amount.
And several more 'rights' on top of these.

But what is 'right?' This is where judgement comes in. The quality of our judgements should develop, the more dilemmas we face and the more decisions we have to make. We learn over time what is more likely to be 'right' through living in the world and truly experiencing it.

In virtue ethics, there are no clear-cut rules that determine what is 'right' and what is 'wrong'. This might seem like a problem for advocates of virtue-based decision making. However, for many of the situations our children face online, there can be no rules – as the situations they face are unique. This means they have to make a character-based judgement. Sometimes this means we have to be lenient and understand that our children will not always make the 'right' judgement. They won't always reason WELL. The important point is what they learn from the experience and that they use it to help them become more reasonABLE.

Of course, developing this quality in our children is easier said than done. To develop reasonableness should be viewed as a lifelong endeavour and one our children need to constantly strive for. It is about learning from when they hit the mark as well as when they miss it.

Our job is to encourage our children to see the quality as being important. It is not to always hold them to account when they make a poor decision. All children will undertake actions with good intentions that don't work out well – this is part of growing up. Some online dilemmas will test them to the limit. After all, their online lives are complex.

Applied reasonableness

Children, young people, in fact all of us face daily dilemmas online. Consider the example below. I have created this dilemma based on my conversations with research participants:

Jack has a homework assignment he has to hand in tomorrow. He has handed in two pieces of homework late recently and will face a detention if he does it again. He has been asked to write a short essay about courage that is to be entered into a national competition. He does some research online and finds a really good short essay on the topic. Although he knows he can't copy it all, he knows he will never be able to write anything better. He can't risk his homework being late again. What should Jack do?

When faced with such a dilemma our children have to show the quality of reasonableness. They have to think through all the actions they might take. While, for this dilemma, the 'right' course of action might seem obvious to us, my guess is it will not be so obvious to our children. The dilemma is more complex than it might first seem. For example, it involves a clash of virtues. Two 'rights' – should Jack be honest or try to show that he is conscientious? Jack might have friends who have faced the same dilemma and 'got away' with the seemingly less virtuous response. Ask your children what they would do if they faced the same dilemma and you will see that the conversation can become complex.

Being reasonABLE is not just about being able to choose the right course of action when virtues conflict or collide. It is also about choosing the right amount of virtue to show. As I mentioned previously, every virtue has a sweet spot. Consider the lists in the following table:

Missing the Mark	Sweet Spot	Missing the Mark
Cowardice	Courage	Rashness
Irritability	Patience	Apathy
Stinginess	Generosity	Wastefulness
Indecisiveness	Self-discipline	Indecisiveness
Self-depreciation	Confidence	Vanity
Meanness	Compassion	Self-sacrifice

You can see that for each of these qualities there is a deficiency and an excess. You can transfer these into online settings, such as imagining what it would look like for your child to hit the sweet spot (or golden mean) of online courage. This would require them to not be cowardly and to stand up to online bullies, but at the same time not be rash by putting themselves or others in danger. Likewise, you don't want your children to be mean to others online, but you also don't want them to be overly self-sacrificing to the detriment of their own health and wellbeing.

I use hypothetical dilemmas in my work because they offer a good way to *cognitively prime* young people. They help them learn which virtue to prioritise and in what amount when faced with a dilemma. Having thought about and worked through some true-to-life dilemmas, children should be better prepared if a similar situation occur in their lives.

Character and being reasonABLE

In a study undertaken by the think-tank Demos, researchers found a relationship between character, online behaviour and decision making.[2] The researchers surveyed nearly seven hundred sixteen- to eighteen-year-olds, to look at how they responded to online ethical scenarios as well as how they self-evaluated their own character strengths. Their research is limited by the usual issues about self-reporting on character, but does provide some food for thought.

The researchers presented three scenarios to the participants, which were designed to reflect commonplace situations on social networking sites. Each scenario was classified in accordance with the threat of harm it posed to the victim and respondent, rising from 'mild' to 'moderate' to 'severe'. The scenarios were:

Mild: 'You write a post arguing for a cause you believe in. Someone comments on it, aggressively disagreeing with your opinion.'

Moderate: 'One of your classmates writes a post insulting someone else in your class, and tags you in it.'

Severe: 'A friend shares an explicit image of someone in your class over social media, and asks you to forward it to another friend.'

Respondents were then asked to say what they would do in each situation and, crucially, why. What the researchers found was fascinating. When presented with an issue, the majority of the teenagers surveyed said they would choose to take a positive course of action (meaning they would attempt to resolve the situation or minimise harm), but many also said they would do nothing. Boys were significantly more likely than girls to say they would do nothing and also almost twice as likely as girls not to recognise a scenario as requiring any kind of moral judgement. What was particularly interesting was that both boys and girls were more likely to take positive action if they knew the person being victimised than if they did not.

The researchers also found that sixteen- to eighteen-year-olds who admit to engaging in risky or unethical behaviour online also demonstrate lower levels of moral sensitivity towards others, and had lower self-reported character qualities. Those who scored 'high' on the self-reported character scores were more likely to 'do the right thing' when faced with a dilemma online – such as being asked to share an explicit image of a classmate. In this example, they would be more likely to tell the person to delete the image and give a reason for doing so (e.g. to protect the feelings of others). Interestingly, those with a higher character score were also more likely to want to 'do the right thing' for unknown others as well as their friends.

What we can learn from this research is that if we help our children develop moral character qualities, they are more likely to reason morally – and not just for the benefit of people they know.

Being reasonABLE

To respond correctly to an online dilemma demands thought and action. Reflection has been covered in the chapter on being thoughtFULL – in the section that explains the 'power of the pause'. But to pause is not always enough. This book is about helping our children navigate their cyber-worlds, not stand back and passively analyse them. That means helping them to participate in the cyber-world, to interact and be actively engaged participants. This requires them to pause, and then in many cases to act.

In summary, to be reasonABLE is to understand that:

- most situations involve several possible courses of action;

- each of these courses of action will make demands on their character;

- they must make a judgement about which is the right action;

- this requires them to think through the character implications of each;

- sometimes this will involve choosing between two virtues;

- sometimes this will involve finding the sweet spot of a particular virtue;

- sometimes this might involve taking no action at all.

If our children understand all the steps above, they are on their way to understanding the mechanics of what it means to be cyber-wise. Although being reasonABLE is not the same as being cyber-wise, it is a necessary first step. It is also a step that all of us can help our children to take.

CHAPTER 13: KEY MESSAGES

- Being reasonABLE is the quality of being able to think through different courses of action when faced with a dilemma and choose the right one to take.

- The right course of action is not always easy to determine, and it depends on the specifics of different situations. Sometimes it will involve having to choose between two virtues – two possible goods.

- Being reasonABLE is not a passive quality – it has cognitive and active parts to it. It is about thinking and doing.

- Research shows that the higher the moral character qualities of children, the more likely they are to choose the moral course of action when faced with an online dilemma.

- Although we can't didactically teach children to be reasonABLE, we can strengthen this quality by exposing our children to hypothetical yet real-life online dilemmas and asking them to think through what they would do. This might be viewed as a form of cognitive priming.

14

Have Integrity

Integrity is a virtue that we talk about all the time, but how often do we stop and think about what it really means? For me, it is a quality that is closely related to being honest, but it is also about a way of life. Put it another way: we talk about people making honest decisions in specific situations. If they are honest consistently, we might describe them as having integrity.

Integrity builds up over time. To have integrity is to have a set of principles that are sustained over a lifetime. It is about being consistently true to one's moral self.

In this chapter I explain how it is important that our children develop an overarching vision of having online integrity. This is the goal. I then show the micro-steps along the way that children must take that build towards this goal. These are related throughout the chapter to core online concerns that test integrity, including fake news, authenticity, plagiarism and anonymity.

It might help you to think in terms of your children walking the path to integrity. This includes them having to:

- visualise the path to integrity – having an authentic vision for how they want to live with integrity online;

- taking the steps to integrity – walking the path towards being regarded as having integrity;

- falling off and getting back on the path to integrity – understanding what to do when things go wrong.

Each of these three areas will be covered in the following pages. First, I want to say more about what it means to live with integrity online.

Integrity as a state of being

Mhairi Black was elected as a Member of Parliament (MP) in 2015. When Mhairi was elected she was the youngest MP to sit in the House of Commons for centuries. Her maiden speech went viral, partly due to her forthright views and her willingness to 'stick it to the man'. Some, though, sought evidence to 'bring her down' and they did not have to look far. They looked at her Twitter timeline. Her tweets included one that said: 'Woke up beside half a can of Tennent's and a full pizza and more money than I came out with. I call that a success!' At the time of posting this, it is unlikely that Mhairi was thinking she would become an MP and that everything she had previously written and posted could and would be used against her. But this tweet and others were used as evidence by some to say that she was not fit and proper to be a Member of Parliament.

Take another case. Paris Brown was appointed as the first youth and crime commissioner in Britain, when she was seventeen years old. Her job did not last long. One week. Paris was dismissed after an investigation into inappropriate tweets she sent when she was fourteen years old – three years before she got the job. As with Mhairi, people were scouring her digital legacy to see if they could use it as evidence that she was not a fit and proper person for the role she had been appointed to.

Although we may not envision our children in such high-profile roles, these tales should make them cautious. What they post on social media and other places online becomes their digital legacy. Take the case of Justine Sacco, who was largely unknown before she posted an ill-advised tweet, just before she boarded a flight to South Africa. Before the plane took off, she posted a few tweets that she obviously thought were funny and that she hoped her 170 followers might also enjoy. According to the *New York Times*,[1] one of these tweets was: 'Going to Africa. Hope I don't get Aids. Just kidding. I'm white!' She then turned off her phone for the flight, unaware of the 'Twitter storm' that was brewing. When Justine landed, she discovered she was the number one trending topic on Twitter in the world. Her tweet was, in most people's eyes, in poor taste, though clearly a parody of racism. However, people had interpreted it as racist and thousands were calling for her to lose her job – and she did. One poorly thought-out comment posted publicly online had dramatically changed her life.

Our children's digital legacy could be sought out and used by anyone in the future. This is why we need our children to construct an authentic vision for how they would like to be viewed in the future and then do everything that they can to build towards or maintain this. The end goal of this vision should be online integrity.

Integrity as the goal for digital legacy is closely linked to identity construction. A person with an identity that is founded on having integrity states clearly what they believe in and then does everything they can to live in accordance with this vision. How do we know if someone is being true to an identity founded on integrity? We know because their actions are widely held to be both good and authentic.

Placing integrity at the heart of our children's digital legacy

Some people might argue that Mhairi, Paris and Justine deserved negative attention as they should have thought before they posted their comments online. I would defend them on the basis that the Internet has not been designed with children or young people in mind. It does not take into account their maturity levels and that it is natural for young people to experiment, to make mistakes and to live in the moment. They have not had time to learn fully about the consequences of their actions. They are not fully wise, meaning they are not always able to look into the future and see how their digital legacy might come back to haunt them.

When we grew up, this was, of course, the same for us. But there is one big difference today. What we said in the heat of the moment was often easily forgotten. What our children write and post online is often preserved. It becomes their permanent digital footprint. The Internet seemingly never forgets.

The first step to our children maintaining a clean and positive digital legacy is to encourage them to see into the future. Did anyone ever sit down with Paris, Mhairi and Justine and ask them fundamental questions such as: 'How do you want people to see you in the future?' Did anyone encourage them to think about how their posts, tweets and other online communication would be used as evidence in how people will judge them? Maybe they did and maybe Paris, Mhairi and Justine's tweets did have integrity as they were true to what they believed in and who they wanted to be at that time. We need to give our children opportunities to seriously think through these big questions. We don't want their integrity to be damaged because we did not help them to see the bigger and longer-term picture.

As parents we need to facilitate this process. We should make the first move. We must help children ask the following questions of themselves:

- What could I do online today that I would be happy to be remembered for?

- What could I do online today that I would *not* want to be remembered for?

The answer to these questions will provide a roadmap to having a digital legacy based on the virtue of integrity. It will provide our children with a goal to aim for. It will help them see that integrity is a state of being and a way of life.

Note that the process starts with asking our children who they want to be. Given their maturity levels, we must help them shape a positive image – through offering exemplars, inspiration and guidance among other things. However, they must ultimately want to become a certain sort of person – this has to come from them. Once they have a vision, they have a goal that should guide all of their online and offline actions and communications.

Children have to be helped to understand that having integrity should be at the heart of their digital identity and that this will become their digital legacy.

Taking steps along the path to integrity

If creating a digital legacy founded on the virtue of integrity is the goal for our children, what are the steps they must take to reach the goal? The bad news is that you can never reach the goal, as all our actions are watched and judged. There will always be times when our children, and indeed all of us, drop some or all of the way back down the integrity path.

In the section below, I detail some of the most likely online traps – the situations in which our children might lose their way on the path to integrity.

Anonymity – operating in the daylight

As our children go about their lives in their cyber-worlds, their integrity is constantly being tested and challenged. This is, of course, also true of their lives in their offline worlds. The difference is that, offline, they almost always have to operate in the open. It is easier to hide online, to be anonymous. When children think they can hide, they sometimes think they can get away with more, as there are fewer checks on their behaviour. This means there are fewer checks to help them stay on their path to integrity.

This is why we must keep reminding our children that integrity is important. If they see having integrity as important, then all of their actions must contribute to it. This means, even if they are anonymous online, they are still seeking to communicate with others with honesty and compassion. In being truthful with others they are also being true to themselves.

Fake news

Fake news is as old as time itself, though it was Collins dictionary 'word of the year' in 2017. Like many things on the Internet, the modern phenomenon of 'fake news' started out as a way to make money. It is believed that the modern idea of fake news began with a group of entrepreneurial young people in one town in Macedonia. The group made up sensational stories so that people clicked through to read them. Clicks, through advertising, translate to cash. Today, there are many reasons why people publish fake news, including a desire to create a culture of suspicion of facts and of experts, spreading fear or anxiety, and the manipulation and influencing of public debate. Fake news is now a global issue that affects all of us.

Children have always made up stories about other people – this is not new. The Internet has brought a new and likely wider audience for these stories. But what is the increasing prevalence of fake news doing to our children's sense of right and wrong? If fake news is seen to be normal, everyday and expected, this will probably make them more cynical and suspicious. People who are seen not to hold a regard for speaking the truth are often thought of as having low or no integrity.

As parents, we have to help our children understand this. We need them to think about whether they are posting truths online. But we also need to help them to be critical, almost suspicious, themselves. They can't take everything at face value. They have to learn to ask questions and make challenges – is everything they read on their timelines and news feeds true? This puts us parents in a difficult position. We don't want our children to live in fear and not believe anything, but at the same time we do need them to be realistic about the nature of modern communication. It is easy to spread miscommunication online and there are powerful economic, political, social and other incentives for doing so.

I suggest we don't start by asking our children to be too fearful or sceptical of other people's communications. What is more important is that they look at their own. Encourage them to question before they post. Do they strongly believe what they are about to post to be true? What is their evidence base for what they are writing? Do they have to post something if they are not sure of its factual basis? What will be the consequences of not posting it?

Asking these questions goes back to their integrity vision. If our children see themselves as someone who others trust, rely on and believe in, then everything they write must contribute to this goal.

Plagiarism

One of the biggest issues that universities are dealing with these days is plagiarism. This has always been an issue for universities – hence the almost fanatical focus on citing, referencing and overall academic integrity. It is a bigger problem than ever before. There are two explanations for this and both have a connection to the Internet. The first is that more students are plagiarising because it is easier than ever to find sources and then copy and paste them. The other reason is that the Internet makes it much easier for universities to catch students plagiarising – software scours the Internet to find sources that are similar to students' submitted work. Either way, the web has weaponised plagiarism.

Plagiarism is a big potential stumbling block for those keen to uphold their integrity. All new students at my university are made to complete what is called an 'academic integrity' course on arrival – it is an attempt to educate them about the dos and don'ts of writing and submitting assignments. Many students still fall foul of the plagiarism checkers and are hauled in front of panels to explain their actions. The explanation that concerns me most is those who say that they did not know it was wrong. Increasingly, young people do not see an issue in copying the best of what they have found online – for some it seems like the most sensible thing to do.

There are two main issues for those who plagiarise. The first is that they are forgoing the chance to have their own voice, to form their own opinions and state what they think about what matters to them. The other is that students will likely lose their integrity in the eyes of others. Students have also been thrown out of university for plagiarism.

Our role, as educators, is to help our children see from an early age that it is important that they develop their own voice. To be authentic and to try to be unique. This is not to say they shouldn't be inspired and draw on other people's ideas and creations – very little is truly 'original'. However, children must learn to be inspired by others and then form their own ideas. These ideas should adhere to their authentic vision – they should have integrity. Our children must realise it is better to fail honestly than to succeed dishonestly. They must look to the longer term and think about how their short-term actions will be viewed. Because it is so easy, online plagiarism really is a trap.

Integrity and identity

The Internet gives children powerful tools with which to craft their identities. These tools can also help our children maintain or destroy their integrity. Given that social media sites work on popularity and attracting followers and friends, it is perhaps not surprising how keen children are to present the best sides of themselves. This might be seen as a process of putting a mask on, one that might gain greater peer affirmation.

The distinguished Harvard academic Howard Gardner and his co-author Katie Davis called this the 'packaged self'.[2] They say that the desire young people have to package themselves online is driven by three interconnected Is: Identity, Intimacy and Imagination. Their argument is that young people seek to self-present online in certain ways and as if they are involved in a form of public performance. This is undertaken in order to drive intimacy with others, which is forged, documented and controlled through the tools that social media provides. What is important here is imagination; the ability to express oneself creatively to gain attention. While, in most cases, Gardner, Davies and others who have written on this topic think that such actions are mainly harmless, they do raise some ethical questions linked to integrity.

The Internet has put rocket boosters under what the sociologist Ernest Goffman called the 'presentation of self'.[3] Goffman's theory was that we are all performers on a stage. When we come into contact with other people, we try to guide the impressions they make of us. We do this by being conscious of our manner, appearance and any other indicators that might tell other people about us.

Goffman was not alive when the Internet was invented, but we can see his ideas writ large in how people use the technology today. In 2017, the most popular paid-for app on the Apple site was 'Facetune'.

This is a selfie editing app that allows users to 'photoshop' their photos before posting them. You can use the app to whiten your teeth, narrow your waist, remove a spot, etc. Considering the popularity of the selfie – it was the word of the year in 2013 – it is not surprising how popular Facetune is. Some surveys have shown that nearly 70 per cent of people edit their selfies before posting them.[4] This includes both men and women.

The question of integrity for our children is a question about how much they are willing to distort 'true' representations of themselves to attract followers. Will their integrity be questioned if they use features of social media to augment those parts of themselves they like and downplay the ones they are less keen on? This is a balance, because we all do this in some form or another on and offline. However, today children have much more powerful tools that allow them to create an identity that isn't true to them. If our children push the limits too far, their authenticity, as well as their integrity, will be likely called into question.

Helping our children when they step or fall off the path to integrity

It's all very well if our children follow the steps along the integrity path and generally make wise decisions. But what happens when they step or fall off it?

We should be prepared for this to happen. We should probably expect it. Our children will get things wrong and make mistakes, just as we did. A good example is one I heard recently from a friend at the school gates. It is about a great kid who goes to school in the local area. He is kind, friendly and has many of the other qualities that we all want our children to possess. Soon after he started secondary school, much to the shock of his parents, he shared a nasty message on WhatsApp about someone in his class. The message got shared round the class. He got into big trouble at home. This communication was out of character. When asked why he did it, he said it was a spur of the moment thing and he was egged on by another friend. He had just got the phone and he had no idea of what his online communication might lead to. He does now.

It was in recognition of these types of actions that the iRights campaign was established in 2015 and has been backed by government ministers in the UK. The campaign has called for under-eighteens to have the right to delete embarrassing and damaging material they have posted on social media that could later harm their future job or education prospects. In Europe, there is regulation enabling adults to demand the removal of any images and text they posted online when they were under the age of eighteen. There are now companies that you can pay to clean up your digital past. These moves acknowledge that we are asking a great deal of our children to predict the long-term consequences of their online actions. This was not something that we were expected to do when we grew up.

There are things that we can do to help our children get back on the path to integrity should they step or fall off it. Here are some suggestions that link to the REACT model.

Rules – if your children are caught posting nasty messages late at night, you might have to (re-)enforce rules. It might be necessary to remove the phone from them in the evening or put a block on their access. Rules do help us all keep our integrity, as they remind us what is expected by society. The hope is that we 'do what is right' without the need for rules, but rules act as useful reminders and also as a good way to 'reset' situations when something has gone wrong.

Exemplar – if your child makes a mistake you might want to remind them of mistakes you have made and what happened as a result of them. I am not always the best at doing this, but I do try to acknowledge my mistakes, take responsibility for any unkindness and do what I can to make it right. In telling these stories to my children, I want them to know two things. First, that I get things wrong – it is part of being human. Second, I want them to know what steps I had to take to try to make things right again.

Advisor – we need to actively support children get back up onto their integrity path. We need to help them think about what they can do to re-establish their integrity, as well as what they might learn about their actions to make it less likely they will repeat them in the future. This might involve asking questions, listening, reminding our children of their integrity vision and advising them on steps they can take to stay on it.

Character champion – having integrity is ultimately about character. The key virtue here is cyber-wisdom. We need children to understand that wisdom is built over time and that, although they might not always get things right, what matters is that they use negative incidents to hone their cyber-wisdom.

CHAPTER 14: KEY MESSAGES

- To have integrity is not about being honest a few times. To have integrity is a lifetime goal – it is to have a set of moral principles that can be sustained over a lifetime.

- We need to help our children develop an online integrity vision, to see acting with honesty and other virtues as a state of being. Maintaining a positive and authentic digital legacy should be at the heart of this vision.

- The path to online integrity has many steps. It also contains many traps along the way. In particular, our children have to watch out for traps connected to identity construction, plagiarism, acting anonymously online and fake news.

- We should expect our children to fall off the path to integrity and be prepared to help them back on it. We can draw on the REACT model to provide guidance on what we can do to help our children regain their online integrity.

15

Be Virtuous

The word virtue, in some places, has got a bad name for itself. It is seen, by some, to be old-fashioned and related to perhaps more austere times. One of my aims in this book is to reclaim the language of virtue and show how it is as relevant today as it has ever been. The book is largely about the virtues children must develop if society is to flourish in the future.

To possess courage, compassion, integrity and other human virtues will enable our children to self-determine the path their lives take. However, I understand that some people are uncomfortable with a term such as virtue. If this more or less describes you, then you might want to swap virtue with a word such as strength, quality, trait, disposition or values. A pedant – or those who are paid to discuss concepts, such as my academic colleagues! – could spend ages explaining why these terms are not interchangeable with virtue, but this book is about practice and therefore you must find the term that you are most comfortable with.

There are two terms that are often used interchangeably with virtue that I and others are against using. The first is 'soft skills'. Virtues are anything but soft. There is nothing soft about being honest, courageous or resilient. The other term is 'non-cognitive skills'. To possess good character is to possess cognitive abilities to make wise decisions – it's what this book is all about. Finally, on both counts, these are not skills (soft or non-cognitive) that we can simply learn through direct instruction; they are hard qualities of character that all of us hopefully develop over a long time.

I have made a case in Parts One and Two of this book as to why character matters and what virtues are important. In the THRIVE model, two virtues – thoughtfulness, linked to being caring and compassionate, and integrity, linked to being honest and authentic – have been singled out for special attention. These virtues are given special attention because my research shows they are the most important for young people to cultivate if they are to navigate their cyber-worlds successfully. This chapter is about all the other important character virtues that children should seek to cultivate if they are to thrive while online.

Four types of virtue

In my role as Director of Education at the Jubilee Centre for Character and Virtues at the University of Birmingham, I helped to develop a framework for character education.[1] This was our calling card when schools and teachers asked us what character education was. Titled *A Framework for Character Education in Schools*, it is still one of the most important publications we have produced. It makes a clear case for why character matters, what it is and how it might be developed. At the heart of the framework is a table that breaks down the virtues into four types and shows how they link together and flow through practical wisdom to contribute to individual and societal flourishing.

Although this four-part typology could be criticised for being too neat, it is not designed to provide a perfect description of human character. It is designed rather to provide a model that helps teachers and parents think about what types of virtue are important and how they fit together. I will describe each of these types and give examples, relating to the Internet, of the virtues in each category we should focus on.

Moral virtues

Moral virtues are extremely important for our children to cultivate if they are to thrive in their cyber-worlds. These are the qualities that build bonds of human trust. We want our children to show kindness and humility to their friends, as we hope their friends will be just and honest in their interactions with our children. When children start to mistrust others online is when the problems start to occur. It is common, for example, for children to act anonymously online. When they start to worry if they can trust the people who are communicating with them, then the common bonds that build friendships break down. It is moral virtues that keep our children feeling that they are part of a rich and positive online (or offline) community.

When moral virtues are not present, the Internet becomes a place where our children worry more and the cyber-world stops being a fun place to live.

This book makes a special case for moral virtues. When everything else has gone, our moral virtues are, I believe, the most important for our children to develop not just online but also offline. The aforementioned *New York Times* columnist, David Brooks, makes this argument better than me. In one of his books, *The Road to Character*, Brooks makes the distinction between 'résumé' virtues and 'eulogy' virtues.[2] He suggests that résumé virtues are the virtues you include on your CV to help you get a job – in the main these will be performance virtues such as leadership, teamwork and adaptability. In contrast, eulogy virtues are those we want people to use to describe us at our funeral. These are largely moral virtues such as compassion, courage and being a loving and caring person. Brooks argues that the pursuit of résumé virtues tends to dominate and, in our doing so, much of what matters and is important about life is forgotten.

In the call to help our children to be virtuous online, the call is for us to help them develop different types of virtues, but, if we are going to focus on any, the moral and intellectual ones might be deemed the most important.

Thoughtfulness as a form of compassion, and integrity as a form of honesty, are the most important moral virtues to develop in our children. These have their own place in the THRIVE model. I also want to make a case for another moral virtue, empathy, which is of particular importance and relates closely to the arguments I make in this book.

Empathy – going the extra mile to consider what others online might be thinking and feeling

Sometimes, the second after I send an email, I start to worry about how what I have written will be interpreted. This worry grows as I keep checking my inbox for a reply and hopefully some relief from my anxiety. Although email has its advantages, it is an inferior form of communication to face-to-face conversations. This is why, when I have something important to say that I want to ensure is understood in the right way, I always pick up the phone or arrange a video or meet in person.

Linguistic research shows us that speech conveys more explicit information than writing. This is because speech gives us more evidence to help us determine meaning. We get clues about what people think and feel through their pitch, rhythm and the stress that is put on particular words. In addition, when we can see the other person, we gain a whole raft of body-language clues. Perhaps most importantly, we get instant and often simultaneous feedback. We are able to catch ourselves mid-sentence and change tack if we feel what we are saying is hurting someone. These affordances are not possible in email exchanges or in instant messaging conversations. This is what the emoji was invented for. We use these to aid communication, to strengthen meaning; they are a visual clue to help the reader understand not just what we are saying but also how we are saying it. The emoji is a guide to our feelings and helps people read us and respond appropriately.

This is why empathy is such an important virtue to develop. For many people, empathy is not an active emotion, such as compassion. When we are compassionate, we actively have to reach out and help others. We can be empathetic without doing anything. However, the quality is vital in the online world. If our children can think about what those they communicate with online might be thinking and feeling, they will be more careful about what they write and send. A good example to demonstrate this is the high number of instances of what might be called accidental cyber-bullying.

In my research I have found countless examples of young people who worry that they have accidently cyber-bullied their friends. They said this is because they could not predict the consequences of a particular form of communication. One thirteen-year-old boy told me that words, written down, can seem much more threatening than when spoken and you can also read and re-read them. In the case of cyber-bullying, some instances might be intentional, and others might be simply a form of miscommunication due to misinterpretation. The increased prevalence of bullying online is likely due to the fact that bullies are shielded from the immediate effects of their bullying online communication as they are hiding behind the keypad.

John Suler called this the 'asynchronicity' effect.[3] This occurs when people communicating online are not faced with the immediate emotional response that might make them check or change their behaviour. There is no immediate feedback loop. For Suler, this is because often the attention is focused on the task, not the recipient, leading to a reduction of cues that aid accountability. In these situations, bullies either can't or don't want to see the consequences of their actions; the latter might be considered a case of wilful blindness. Research has shown that young people bully others online because it makes them feel as though they are funny, popular, and powerful, although many indicate feeling guilty afterwards.[4] What makes bullying through online communication particularly pernicious is that the perpetrators are protected from the immediate effects of their actions.

This is why empathy is so important. It is an attempt to see situations from other people's points of view and decide on a course of action accordingly. Examples of other moral virtues that children should enact online include:

- Courage – reaching out to others who you can see are being bullied online, even if your friends might bully you for doing so.

- Humility – not thinking less of yourself online but trying to think more of others by supporting their positive online actions.

- Gratitude – being thankful for having the technology that

allows you to make so many connections and stay in touch with friends. Showing this gratitude by using the technology as a tool to improve others' lives.

Performance virtues

If moral virtues were what people associated character with in the past, today character is most commonly associated with performance virtues. For example, sports players are often described in terms of their character in news stories. Occasionally, the reporters are talking about their integrity, but normally they are talking about their resilience, determination and leadership among other qualities. In schools, performance virtues are also prominent – teachers often pride themselves on running activities that develop teamwork or perseverance. They are normally the qualities that young people are encouraged to put on their CVs and that are described by teachers in personal statements.

The truth is that although these virtues probably gain the most attention in today's world, most of us don't think they are as important as moral virtues. This is because, strictly speaking, they are not really virtues. They don't necessary equate to human goodness. Being determined or a good leader might get you ahead in life, but it might not be good for those around you. It is only when these qualities are used to enhance moral, civic and intellectual virtues that they actually become human 'goods'. We want our children to show determination when they are being egged on by their mates to post an embarrassing picture of their friend online. The 'good' here is not the determination, but the compassion they feel for their friend who they don't want to embarrass. The performance virtues need to be applied to the other types of virtues if they are to be truly valuable.

This is why none of the virtues in the THRIVE model fall into the performance category. As a parent, I want my children to cultivate these qualities, but they are not necessary, on their own, to become cyber-wise and a good cyber-citizen.

Resilience is good – but for what?

We probably hear more about resilience than any other character quality these days. Policy makers, teachers, parents and others often say that we need to build up the resilience of our children. Lack of resilience is blamed for many things, from mental health to youth unemployment. It has become a buzzword of our age.

I think that resilience is important to develop in our children – but it is often misunderstood as a quality. What are we actually developing resilience for? It has to be tied to an end and, ideally, a good end. After all, many online hackers are probably resilient, but their behaviour is not ethical. I believe we need our children to develop resilience so that they can demonstrate moral, civic and intellectual virtues even when the going gets tough. In this sense, resilience is a muscle – it makes things happen but is not necessarily a good in itself.

On the Internet, we need children to be resilient in a variety of situations. First, when they have fallen off the integrity path. It takes resilience to get back up, learn from the experience and move on when you have been caught sending nasty messages to other people over social media. We need children to show resilience when they are trying to set up an online charity event that is taking time to get off the ground. They need to show resilience when they receive nasty messages about a picture or post. They need to show perseverance and rebound from setbacks when their ideas don't seem to be working. To be an exemplar to others takes resilience, particularly when peer pressure is involved. These are just a few examples of where resilience matters in the online space that many children operate in. Importantly, all these examples are connected to other moral, civic and performance virtues.

Civic virtues

Civic virtues can be seen as the public expression of good character. In the online world, this means seeking out opportunities to be positive, engaged, participatory and active cyber-citizens.

The amplification of civic virtues was one of the aspirations of the early pioneers of the Internet. Their hope was that the Internet would unite people around positive causes, that it would bring people together to tackle global concerns. For our children to display civic virtues online, they must see the Internet as a tool that can enhance human understanding, compassion and connections around the world. They must see the Internet as a technology to fight local, national and international injustice. As a tool that amplifies their voice to fight for good causes. This means using social networks to build alliances around issues that matter – be they climate change or reducing cyber-bullying in a school.

Civic virtues are closely related to online civility. We hear often that social media is the home of online hate and human unpleasantness. The Internet has been described as a cesspit. This is because people do not always communicate with civility. That does not mean agreeing with what everyone says – it is more about how you disagree.

The technology becomes truly powerful and potentially life-changing when it is used by people who are civically minded, civically active and possess virtues that are directed at helping others.

eService – reaching out to help others online

Service, like the term virtue, is sometimes viewed as an antiquated word or connected with the military or being servile. At its simplest, service is the action of helping other people. I believe we need more children and young people who look out for opportunities to help others. The idea of service is at the heart of national campaigns and programmes like the National Citizen Service and Step up to Serve. It was part of the vision, from the outset, of the Scouts, Guides and many other local and national activities that children engage in.

Many of these organisations are continuing to support children and young people in helping others through the use of technology and, in particular, the Internet. They are promoting what might be called eService. This has to be real and not tokenistic – it also has to involve real thinking and real doing. eService is not clicking the 'like' button on a charity campaign without researching what is behind it. It needs to be more than this. It is about using Internet tools actively to reach out to help others online.

One of the greatest affordances the Internet offers us all is an opportunity to connect with people who don't live close by. Great eService projects are often about building great human relationships, bringing people together around shared ideas and ideals. eService projects might simply digitalise actions that currently take place offline, to amplify them and broadcast them to new audiences. There are hundreds of examples of citizenship projects that take place daily through community groups, charities and schools. Encourage your children to be inspired by these projects and find ways they can use their digital skills and the power of the Internet to increase the scope and likely impact of them. For example, they could offer to build or improve a website for a local charity, or run an online fundraising campaign.

Engaging in eService is also a great activity for the whole family. It offers a chance to unite around a project that seeks to make a difference. The ideal family eService project would:

1. Have a role for all the family and build on everyone's strengths. For example, one of your children may be a whizz with the computer and another might be super-creative. You might be able to bring knowledge of project management and budgeting. The project should be an opportunity to learn from each other.

2. Be active. To make it truly educational it needs to be a project that requires some research to set it up and some effort to carry it out. A good project would require everyone to be proactive, innovative and entrepreneurial.

3. Be real. In today's online world it would be possible to set up a whole fantasy project, using avatars in an alternative online world. This might be fun, but it is much better if the project is about real people and real issues. It is in the real world that our character is truly tested.

4.   Involve some critical reflection. Ask questions like, why have we decided to support this cause? What went well and what might we do differently next time?

5.   Inspire. There are not many people undertaking family eService projects. Be the first in your area to do so and you will no doubt inspire others to do the same.

Intellectual virtues

Intellectual virtues are what enable our children to successfully enact the other three types of virtues. Practical (or cyber-) wisdom is an intellectual virtue. It might be said to be the master virtue, as it orchestrates all the others. Other intellectual virtues are just as important to cultivate in our children, who are more likely to possess independent authentic character if they are able to be critical, autonomous thinkers. This means that they are able to look at different situations and independently make a judgement about what is the best thing to do. We, as parents, must help our children by giving them some context, boundaries, advice and structure, but also space for them to make sense of these in their own way. The intellectual virtues help them to pursue knowledge, truth and understanding. They are required for independent learning. Think of virtues such as curiosity, open-mindedness and resourcefulness – they are also required for deeper learning. Think of virtues such as critical reflection.

If our children possess these qualities, they are more likely to thrive online. They will be able to question the integrity of messages and posts and evaluate their meaning. They will be able to see alternative points of view and not take everything they read online as the truth. They will be able to judge what is the 'right' thing to do when responding to a social media post. They will be able to pause, slow things down and take time for reflection. They are less likely to be hot-headed. They won't always respond in an instant. Intellectual virtues are vital for 'good' online action.

Cyber-wisdom – bringing it all together

This book has largely been about one particular intellectual virtue: cyber-wisdom. It is this virtue, above all others, that I believe is the most important for us to seek to cultivate in children and young people. Put simply, if we all act with more wisdom online, the real and cyber-worlds will be better places to live.

The crucial qualities at the heart of wisdom are critical discernment and judgement. Cyber-wisdom is about making the right call about which virtue is required in a particular situation. It arbitrates between the moral, civic, performance and other intellectual virtues. If we have cyber-wisdom we know when to be loyal to a friend and when to report their online wrongdoing.

Cyber-wisdom, above all other virtues, is the intellectual virtue that online human flourishing depends on. Examples of other intellectual virtues that children should enact online include:

Critical thinking – not taking what you read online as true, and checking multiple sources.

Broad-mindedness – being responsive to new opportunities that come to you through your timeline or news feed and particularly those that seem to help others and improve the cyber-world.

Open-mindedness – being open to different viewpoints you are exposed to online. Going beyond the online echo chamber.

Curiosity – going outside of your usual online friends to seek out other opinions, ideas and ways of doing things.

Becoming virtuous

Of the virtues listed above, we should pay particular attention to the moral, civic and intellectual. This is because they are particularly important for children and young people to possess if they are to live successfully alongside others online. These virtues might be seen as the glue that binds people together and they indicate that we consider how our actions affect others. Although the performance virtues receive a great deal of attention in the media and public policy, they are seen as less vital for a society to thrive, perhaps more related to individual flourishing. More importantly, they might be said to be amoral. Criminals as well as Nobel Peace Prize winners both possess these qualities.

It is the virtues and how we champion them that will ultimately determine how our children use the Internet. This will determine if they engage in risky or unethical behaviours or use the technology for laudable and pro-social behaviours. While they are ultimately the masters of their destinies, where they end up depends on the decisions they make. These decisions or judgements depend in turn on what they know and understand and believe to be right and true. This all comes down to the virtues they possess – including cyber-wisdom as the master of them all.

In the last part of this book I provide practical activities that seek to cultivate the four types of virtues required for living well online.

CHAPTER 15: KEY MESSAGES

- Thoughtfulness (to be compassionate and caring) and integrity (to be honest and authentic) are the two most important virtues to seek to cultivate in our children if they are to THRIVE online. This chapter is about all the other virtues that are important. These will determine if our children act ethically or unethically online.

- Moral virtues are the bonds that build human trust. Empathy is a moral virtue that is a particularly important virtue in the online age. If our children can think about what other people might be thinking and feeling, they will be more careful about what they post on social media. Other important moral virtues include courage, humility and gratitude.

- Performance virtues (or qualities) such as resilience and teamwork are not good in themselves – they become 'good' when they are tied to the moral, civic or intellectual virtues. Resilience will help children bounce back from challenging situations they might find themselves in online.

- Civic virtues help children communicate with others successfully online; they are essential for being responsible digital citizens. An expression of digital citizenship would be to set up an eService project – using technology to reach out and help others.

- Intellectual virtues are what help children put the other virtues into action – they require independent autonomous moral thinking as well as the pursuit of knowledge, truth and understanding. The most important of the intellectual virtues is practical wisdom. Open-mindedness, critical thinking and curiosity are other important intellectual virtues.

16

Be an Exemplar

If our children . . .

- are **T**houghtful and thoughtFULL;
- remember to act with **H**umanity online;
- are **R**easonABLE;
- have **I**ntegrity;
- and act **V**irtuously

. . . then they will be good exemplars to others.

Given the reach of the Internet, they could be an inspiration to their friends but also to people they don't know around the world. They could also be an exemplar to you.

They may also be parents themselves one day and be an exemplar to their children, thus creating a virtuous circle, passing around and down the knowledge of a character-based approach to flourishing online.

Growing up and growing wise: Our children as the exemplars

The importance I place on exemplars for the cultivation of cyberwisdom should be obvious. It is the only quality to feature in both the REACT and THRIVE models. This is because so much character development occurs through what might be considered a form of osmosis. We form our ideas, principles and values based on those around us. People inspire us to behave well or badly. We assimilate virtues often without knowing it.

It is important that our children perceive themselves as exemplars. They must know and understand that their actions will be observed and copied by those around them. They have a role in setting the expectations for others. It is our responsibility to remind our children regularly about this.

I know the ideal I am calling for is not easy, particularly given the pressure most children experience from their peers growing up. For our children to stand up for something they think is right takes courage. Many children I interviewed said they had been involved with saying nasty things to others online because their friends encouraged them to. They did not lead, but they followed without too much resistance. To be an exemplar takes thought. It is about leading, not following.

If we can encourage our children to see themselves as exemplars in their online actions, this will also have a longer-term and important effect. The effect will be across the generations. If a whole generation were to learn to use the Internet more wisely, this would change the norms and expectations for its use. This is what Tim Berners-Lee called for when he said we must all be involved in efforts to make the cyber-world a place in which we want to live.

What can we do?

Apart from being the best possible exemplars ourselves, here are some other actions we can take. We can:

- Try not to make too-high demands on our children to act as exemplars to others. There is only so much they can do on their own and they are also likely to get things wrong. These struggles should be seen as part of the narrative of their lives.

- Show our children that exemplars are often people who stand out from the crowd and try to do things differently. We can encourage them to look at how Greta Thunberg responded to trolls to gain greater support for her environmental campaign and how Lizzie Velásquez was inspired by online 'haters' to launch her own anti-bullying campaign.

- Remind our children it is never too late. Some of the best-known exemplars are people who have lived troubled or challenging lives and turned them round. Their stories are often heroic and draw us in. They also have resonance. They replicate what life is like in the 'real' world. They are rich stories, full of detail. They are not black and white; they have grey areas. These are the truer and more human exemplars.

- Try not to have too-high demands on our children to act or behave exactly like one of their friends whom we admire. There is no such thing as the 'cookie-cutter' exemplar, the role model that all shall follow. Children are unique and too complex for this. It is our children's idiosyncrasies and their imperfections that make them special to us.

- Inspire our children by sharing fictional exemplars, those that feature in books or films. These might serve to inspire and show our children the art of the possible, but we should not force our children to be like them. This has to come about more naturally. There is no blueprint for character development and therefore we can't expect people to act and behave exactly like others. Perhaps just as importantly, we might find encouraging children to behave like virtuous exemplars has the opposite effect, what might be called moral overstretching. If our children feel they cannot live up to or replicate someone we admire, they might instead play down, rebel and reject our advice.

- Ask questions, as most of the time our children will be exemplifying particular behaviours when we are not watching, either over the Internet or when they are at school and with their friends. We can remind them about the importance of setting an example in these situations by asking them questions like:

— How do you think other people would describe your
relationship with your phone?

— Are you a follower or a leader online?

— Do you think you act the same online as offline?

— Have you been embarrassed about a post you have
written that others have forwarded on?

— Tell me something you have done online that has made a
difference to someone else.

— Tell me something you have done online that you are
embarrassed about and why.

The best exemplars inspire us. They strengthen the best bits about us
and our children. They provide impetus for us to seek to shape or change
ourselves when necessary. They show us what is humanly possible and
the different paths to this. They help us to build habits or bolster those
we already possess.

Imagine your child being an active contributor to a new
generation of children who thrive in cyberspace and in doing so show a
path that others can follow.

CHAPTER 16: KEY MESSAGES

- If our children become exemplars to others online, this creates a virtuous circle – their knowledge and behaviour will not just be passed on to others around them but also passed through the generations.

- Being an exemplar is not easy in the face of peer pressure. Our children will also get things wrong. These struggles should be recognised and become part of their exemplar narrative.

- There is no such thing as a cookie-cutter exemplar – it is our children's idiosyncrasies, their imperfections as well as their perfections, that make them special to us.

- Find opportunities to introduce to your children exemplars that you find inspiring, but ensure you do so in a way that does not have the opposite effect and put them off.

Summary of Part Three:
Are Your Children Thriving
or Surviving?

THRIVE is an acronym for the human qualities that children need to possess if they are to successfully negotiate the challenges the digital world presents them. For children and young people to develop these qualities takes time, effort, thought and experience. However, the rewards of cultivating them are great, both for individuals and for society more broadly.

Developing these qualities will make it more likely that they, as well as those around them, will flourish. To thrive is to blossom, grow, prosper, shine and succeed. It is an aspiration to aim for.

The THRIVE model places a specific focus on virtues and other qualities that might be said to be particularly important for young people to possess when they are using cyber-technologies. These are:

- **To be thoughtful**. This must be understood in two ways: to be thoughtful, as in being caring and compassionate; and to be thoughtFULL, as in to be reflective.

- **To be human** is a call for our children to take control of technologies before the technologies take control of them.

- **To be reasonABLE** is to understand that children face daily dilemmas, big and small, when they interact in the cyber-world. These dilemmas call for them to make judgements, to think through their ethical contours, to be critical and to act with reason. Being reasonABLE is a vital component of cyber-wisdom and develops over time as our children become more accomplished at negotiating the ethical conflicts that are thrown at them.

- **To have integrity** is for children to have an overarching understanding of how they want to live in their cyber-worlds in an honest and authentic way. It is about them having consistency and coherence – their behaviour remains the same regardless of context.

- **To be virtuous** is to possess moral, civic, intellectual and performative human qualities that contribute to the leading of good digital lives. These virtues, which might also be called human qualities, strengths, dispositions or traits, are the basis for a happy and flourishing life.

- The final component is a call to be an **exemplar**. This is what is required to create a virtuous circle. By the time our children reach secondary school, they are influenced by their peers more than anyone else. Being an exemplar is a call to pass on their cyber-wisdom to others around them. It is to do this through their actions as much as their words. It is also much more than this; it is about them passing their cyber-wisdom on to future generations, including their own children.

Thriving is an aspiration for the future, but the work towards it starts now.

Cultivating Character and Cyber-wisdom

17

Cultivating Cyber-wisdom through Character Education

Throughout the preceding chapters I have explained each of the components of the REACT and THRIVE models. In doing so, I have provided some activities and lots of advice on what we might do to apply the models in our daily lives. Many of the approaches I have suggested fall into the category of implicit education – things that we might do with our children without too much planning, forethought or structure. My intention so far has not been to provide a curriculum for how you can go about developing character and cyber-wisdom. This is what I turn to in this final part of the book.

While I can't provide you with a set of lessons that will guarantee your children develop cyber-wisdom, I can detail educational strategies and activities that will make it more likely they will develop this quality. I believe we need to be more intentional in some aspects of our education of cyber-wisdom, as the absence of such explicit approaches has left a vacuum. In this chapter I want to set the scene for the educational activities that follow by first explaining that we have been somewhat remiss when it comes to focusing on character education, and then exploring the reasons why this might be. I will subsequently explain how the revival of character education can be a remedy.

The case I want to make is that we have not, on the whole, taught our children very well about how to deal with living in the cyber-world. Most of us do not adopt a conscious, planned and intentional educational approach to educating our children to be better cyber-citizens. I believe, as previously stated, that governments and Big Tech companies have responsibilities to ensure the cyber-world is a world we want our children to live in. In this chapter I also focus on what we can do as parents and teachers.

I argue that while it is parents' responsibility to educate their children to act responsibly in the digital world, if we do not do this job well it will impact on the life and work of teachers. Further, children spend so long in school that teachers have an important role to play in the formation of their character. Schools, or more accurately teachers, shape character.

In the following section I will sketch out the reasons why we might have taken our eye off the ball and what we might do about it.

Parents as the primary educators

How often do you really think about what you are offering your children in the way of education to help them manage the awesome power of their smartphone?

There are some good reasons why we, as parents, might not have been explicit and intentional in educating our children to live with wisdom and character in the cyber-world. Reasons we might give include:

- Lack of knowledge about what to do or how cyber-technologies work.

- Lack of recognition about the risks and opportunities that the cyber-technologies bring with them.

- Paralysis because the problems seem too big and complicated.

- Lack of time with our children to address the issues properly.

- A hope that someone else will do the job better than we can.

Up until my daughter got her first smartphone, I suppose I assumed that educating for cyber-citizenship and cyber-wisdom would fall into the category of what might be called 'intuitive parenting'. When the time came, I thought I would just know what to do. I think I was also guilty of thinking that my children's teachers would pick up the pieces if I did not hit the mark.

As a parent, I should be the one who hurts if my child is found to be bullying someone else online, just as I should be the one who can take some pride if my child sets up a fundraising campaign online to help a local cause. As a parent, I am the primary architect, particularly in their early years, of my children's character. We must teach a child to share, to be fair, to show compassion to others in the early years – and as a parent we have more influence over our children than anyone else at this time.

So, the important question is: what do I or my fellow parents do in the way of educating for cyber-flourishing? How can we be more intentional and more explicit in our approach? If we believe that the development of our children's character is too important to leave to chance, we need to get tougher with ourselves on these questions.

Of course, we still need to educate spontaneously, using our initiative and instinct – grabbing the so-called 'teachable moment'. We are, however, likely to educate in these moments more effectively when our approach is well thought through. This will help to ensure we are consistent and our children do not receive mixed messages. How we do this is likely to be different for each family. There is no magic bullet or one-size-fits-all approach. No script exists that guides us through how best to educate our children's character to help them successfully and morally negotiate their cyber-worlds. I have suggested that the REACT and THRIVE models provide a remedy to this problem. In this part of the book I also suggest a set of structured and explicit teaching and learning activities, many of which are suitable for parents to use, that provide a language and set of tools for character development.

Teachers as character educators

There are some good reasons teachers might give for not adopting a greater focus on character and character education in their teaching.

These include:

- Education has largely been driven by policy in recent years. There have not been any clear-cut policies on character education and the Internet, which has resulted in a lack of impetus and in any suitable and clear advice for teachers.

- Concerns about the competency of teachers to tackle the potentially challenging topic of character, especially since many of the concerns relate to what happens in the home. In addition, teachers receive little training in character education.

- Lack of curriculum time given over to the topic, resulting from an over-focus on assessed subjects in many schools.

Despite these reasons, the national curriculum in the UK offers some teaching on what is often called digital citizenship, largely through Personal, Social, Health and Emotional (PSHE) education. Teachers reading this book will realise that this is a largely maligned subject that does not have enough time or space in the curriculum given the importance of the topics it covers. Other initiatives, such as Safer Internet Day,[1] punctuate the school year and bring some important, if sporadic, visibility to the topic. Schools are increasingly waking up to the issue and offering parents' meetings, assemblies and professional development activities that address it. The response tends to be reactive and to address concerns as they arise – such as cyber-bullying and gaming addiction. It also often focuses on the concerns themselves rather than the desirable character qualities that would make the concerns less of an issue.

One reason why subjects such as PSHE and Citizenship are seemingly languishing is that they are overshadowed by the giants of the curriculum: maths, English and science. How have we decided that our collective health, wellbeing and societal flourishing is less important than our children being able to add up or know what a fronted adverbial is (this really is tested in the Key Stage 2 SATs tests)?

I am being slightly facetious here to make a point. My point is not to knock subjects like maths and English, as they are clearly important. But are they more important than our children being happy and healthy? It is understandable that some teachers believe it is not the responsibility of schools to educate for cyber-citizenship. However, if this education is not taking place in homes, then I believe it is important that schools and teachers have a role. Also, I think many parents, in the absence of other advice, take their lead from schools. Schools, to some extent, have a responsibility to fill this vacuum.

One outcome of PSHE, Citizenship and other subjects that focus on cyber-citizenship being given more status is that parents might also start to take them more seriously. Instead, we seem to be going backwards. The citizenship education experiment in England has not taken off as hoped: not many schools actively prioritise the subject today. PSHE is a non-statutory subject in primary schools, meaning that they are not required to teach it (although some content is statutory) but are encouraged to. The content of the subject is continuously contested, and discussion tends to focus on contentious issues. Why does it not focus more on issues that we tend to agree on? There is broad cultural agreement, across people of faith and no faith that virtues of good (cyber-) citizenship such as wisdom, compassion, honesty, generosity, integrity and others matter.

I understand teachers who tell me that character education should not be their responsibility; they have enough on their plate. Unfortunately, although this is probably true, teachers can't avoid the role. All teachers are character educators whether they like it or not. The only valid question is: are they reflective and intentional character educators? If teachers get character education right, then it should not be another thing on their plate but the plate itself. A plate that everything else rests upon. This includes desirable educational outcomes, such as improved behaviour and attainment,[2] as well as cyber-citizenship. It should be win-win.

Tests of life or life of tests?

Recent educational policy has led teachers away from a focus on character education and parents have largely followed. Today it seems that education is more about preparing young people for a life of tests rather than the tests of life.

Every year surveys show that teachers, parents, employers and the wider public all think that character is more important than attainment.[3] However, character education has never made as many headlines as schools that fail, or are praised, because of their exam results. When politicians talk about schools, they invariably talk about attainment and progress. Academic standards, not character, has been the only game in town for many years. In many ways our school systems have become increasingly marketised. School league tables, based largely on pupil results, have forced schools to compete against each other. Heads roll when schools fall down the tables. So, how do some head teachers respond? They narrow the curriculum and focus only on what they think will bring short-term improvements in attainment. They cancel the art or volunteering club in favour of extra maths or English classes. What inference do our children take from this? That attainment is all that matters. This is what they are ultimately being judged on.

Pisa tables can't tell us everything about a country's education, league tables can't tell us everything about the qualities of a school, and exam results most definitely don't tell us everything about the qualities of our children.

League tables are largely based on measures of attainment. Why? Partly because attainment is the easiest thing to measure. But attainment is only half the educational picture. Should we not also be seeking to judge schools on everything that we value? Character has seemingly been left behind in the push to improve academic standards. I do not think this has been a deliberate policy move by our Ministers for Education, but it is an unintended consequence of their changes to policy. As they sought to improve attainment in maths, English, science and other subjects, they forgot for a while to remind teachers to continue to pay attention to what improved attainment requires – good character. They sought to build higher houses but neglected the foundations.

Good character and a well-honed practical wisdom are the basis for achieving so many other things in life, which is more important in my view than attainment. It is the basis to living happy, connected, flourishing lives. Good character and enhanced cyber-wisdom are part of this picture.

The fact is that this point has been seemingly forgotten. It is easy to fall into the trap and look at our children's education solely through the lens of what their teachers say about them in the reports that are brought home. If we narrow our focus to attainment and grades, we are left with an impoverished definition of education. I believe that a true definition of education has to include the cultivation of human character qualities.

Central to this definition, for me, is the cultivation of practical wisdom in our children and young people. This requires all of us to rewrite the education system – place character development for human online and offline flourishing at the heart of it.

We need to think again about what we believe the purpose of education should be.

The times they are a-changin'

After thirty years of fairly relentless innovation in education in the UK, most of it focusing on the standards agenda, there are early signs that things are changing. In England this started with mentions of character in a Labour white paper on education, which has been extended by the Conservatives in recent years. Most importantly, in 2019 character and character education became one of the judgement criteria in a revised Ofsted framework. Ofsted are the government body responsible for inspecting schools in England – so what they say matters.

In the early 2000s the Labour Party began the process of discussing the importance of character. It also introduced citizenship education as a statutory subject in schools in England. I believe that you can't be a good citizen without having 'good' character – the two are linked. By 'good' citizen I do not mean someone who is compliant and unquestioning. I mean someone who is seeking to make the place they live – be that on a local, national or global level – better for themselves and for others. This does mean speaking up about injustices and campaigning against politicians or institutions when things are unfair. To do this well takes some important character qualities such as compassion for others and a desire for justice. It takes courage to stand up for what you think is right. Debates around what is fair and just are also more likely to be civil and progress if all parties are demonstrating qualities of tolerance and respect for different viewpoints. Citizenship, I believe, should be the outward display of people's inner character qualities.

Perhaps the most significant change is the interest in character that Ofsted has shown. It is currently not possible for schools to receive a good or outstanding judgement unless they can show how they are developing the character qualities of their students. This trend towards more explicit character education is being echoed in many other countries, creating more of a global movement. For example, in the 1980s in the USA the Republicans saw the potential for character education to restore a sense of order and improve behaviour in schools. In the years that followed, this was picked up and redefined by Democrat President Bill Clinton. As in England, the focus on character education has come from the political right and the left.

Perhaps more noticeable is research on character that has become increasingly visible and underpins many popular books on the subject. This includes, notably, Martin Seligman and Chris Peterson's focus on character strengths as the core component of the positive psychology movements. In books such as *Flourish* and *Character Strengths and Virtues*,[4] Seligman and his co-authors argue why a focus on character is so important for our happiness and wellbeing. Other world-famous authors, such as Carol Dweck, also adopt a character-focused approach. Dweck's work on mindsets is essentially an argument that we need to display certain character qualities if we are truly to grow. Take, for example, this quote from Dweck's book about the virtue of courage and mindsets.

> True self-confidence is the courage to be open – to welcome change and new ideas regardless of their source. Real self-confidence is not reflected in a title, an expensive suit, a fancy car, or a series of acquisitions. It is reflected in your mindset: your readiness to grow.[5]

It is worth noting that many countries in Asia are also increasingly interested in character education. For example, the Singapore curriculum, widely believed to be one of the best in the world, rests entirely on concepts of character and citizenship.

Character education, in recent times and around the world, is mostly talked about in connection with schools. As I have been arguing, I think that character development is the responsibility of us all and especially those of us who are parents. This does not mean I go about calling myself a character educator, but frankly this is what I am. My hope is that the increased policy and institutional focus on character and character education will filter through to parents and families, and remind us of what most of us take to be true: that character is what will truly determine our children's happiness and wellbeing.

We all need to think about character more consciously. To consider, what is our responsibility to cultivate character? To ask, what am I doing that might positively or negatively influence the character virtues that my children develop? These are hard questions to ask of ourselves, but they are important ones.

Next steps

In reading the sections above, you might think that we have made little attempt in recent years to cultivate cyber-wisdom in our children. This is clearly not true, and in many schools I visit, I see examples of excellent practice. Several parents I know do make explicit attempts to educate their children to be better users of their smartphones and tablets. When I ask them what approach they are taking, their answers are often muddled. This is not their fault, for when we intentionally educate for cyber-wisdom, we often seem to be scampering around in the dark, not sure of the best way forward. No single approach is adopted and often education is left to teachers trying to find resources (perhaps somewhat ironically) on the Internet.

To ensure education in this space is character-rich, parents and teachers must find the time and discover better tools to help them with the task. In the concluding two chapters of this book I will explain, in practical terms, how character and cyber-wisdom can be explicitly developed through a greater focus on character education.

CHAPTER 17: KEY MESSAGES

- There are a number of reasons why parents and teachers have sometimes neglected to undertake more explicit approaches to education for character and cyber-wisdom. This has left a vacuum that can be addressed.

- One reason for this vacuum is a focus on testing and exams, which has narrowed the curriculum and meant we have forgotten a wider and more important purpose of education: to enhance human flourishing.

- There are signs of hope as politicians in the UK and globally are reawakening to the importance of character education.

- This is an opportunity for educational activities that intentionally and reflectively seek to cultivate character and cyber-wisdom in the interests of online thriving, to be integrated into formal and less formal curriculums.

- Parents and teachers can be intentional in their approach to educating for cyber-citizenship. The education of character, and cyber-wisdom, should be the main focus of any deliberate educational activities.

- A reinvigorated focus on character in both formal and less formal education will bring benefits not just for our children but also for society more broadly.

Pedagogical Approaches to Developing Cyber-wisdom

My intention in this book has not been to make a case for character education per se. Instead, I want to show you how an increasingly widely accepted view of character education might underpin strategies that we can adopt to cultivate cyber-wisdom in our children.

Before I detail activities that develop cyber-wisdom, I will give an overview in this chapter of some of the tried and tested pedagogical approaches to character education that these rest upon. Although no character-building activity is known to work with all children in all situations, research and practice since the millennium have provided some guidelines on what is more likely to work with most children.

Character education is not a form of indoctrination

The recent policy focus on character education is not without its critics, but the arguments tend to be more about *how* it is taught than *why* it is taught. Few people argue that it is important that children understand that human qualities matter. Where arguments exist about the inclusion of character education in schools, they tend to focus on a concern about indoctrination – i.e. how children are introduced to notions of character and what methods are used to encourage them to act in desirable ways.

As I have tried to explain, an approach to character education that encourages individual autonomy, critical reasoning and reflection should not be too contentious. Character education, when delivered well, should support children to reflect on their strengths and weaknesses and assess their actions and behaviour, with a view to moderating them if required. Below is a list of some key questions you might ask yourself if you think your approach might be over-indoctrinating:

- Do your children have a genuine voice in discussions about their behaviour, or do you just tell them how to behave?

- When you listen to your children, are you being tokenistic or are you being authentic – i.e. do you sometimes act on what they say?

- Do you manage your children's behaviour only through rewards and punishments, or do you also encourage them to try to act well because they think it is the right thing to do?

- Do you allow your children to make mistakes and see these as learning opportunities?

- When your children have done something wrong, do you let them speak first and explain their actions, or do you always speak first?

- Do you tell your children there is a right and wrong answer in every situation, or do you tell them that sometimes they have to make a judgement based on their own wisdom?

- Do you allow your children to challenge your views and teach them how to do so in a way that is constructive and positive?

Character can be caught and taught, but always aim for character sought

It is useful to think about character as being taught and caught, but ideally it should be sought.[1] I'll explain why.

Caught . . .

Character, for most people, is largely caught. If I asked you how you developed your character, I would be amazed if you said, 'I learnt it at school.' This is because you can't *teach* character or even one of the virtues, say integrity, in a lesson or series of lessons. We develop our character primarily through a form of osmosis. It was shaped by the core values that surrounded us as we grew up. This is why I have talked so much about exemplars in this book.

But what if an environment that our children grow up in does not always prioritise the sorts of values that we prize? What if they are not surrounded by good exemplars? For example, what if we think our children are being influenced negatively by the people they interact with online? Then we might need to think more about character taught.

. . . taught . . .

Character can also be taught. I don't mean through lessons on, say, honesty or resilience. I mean through more explicit, planned and structured activities that provide children with a language and tools for their own character development. Explicit approaches help children understand why character and cyber-wisdom are important. They also provide children with some tools to help them develop these qualities.

All of the activities listed in the next chapter are a form of character taught. They can be delivered in a planned and conscious way by parents and teachers. Some are more formal in nature; more like lesson plans. Others are more informal, such as ideas for conversation starters.

. . . and sought

Character sought is what we all should be aiming at. To seek out something is to desire it. It is to take ownership of it, to see it as part of one's identity. Things that are desired and freely chosen tend to be more authentic and genuine. This is character sought, when our children choose to act in a particular way, to try to be a particular sort of person.

When our children choose independently to show virtues such

as compassion and honesty in certain situations, it demonstrates they want others to see them as being compassionate and honest people. They want to make these qualities part of their identity. They are making a statement that character, in their eyes, is important and that they are prepared to work to try to 'do the right thing', even when it is hard. Even when no one is watching.

This should be the ultimate aim of character education: to provide the environment, resources, support and motivation that makes it more likely that our children will seek out opportunities, on their own, to be virtuous.

Don't get too hung up on trying to measure your children's character growth

Character is complex. I know this, as I have tried to explain to parents, teachers and policy makers how hard it is to measure.

I am often asked at the end of a talk about how we might measure character. This is a reasonable question. If I have given a one-hour talk on why character education is important and should be a part of all schooling, it is perhaps right to ask how we know that it makes a difference.

I have two answers to this question. My first answer might be seen as a bit of a cop-out, but actually it has depth. I'll say, 'Should we only value and therefore educate what we can measure?' I'll challenge the questioner by asking, 'Should we not also seek to educate in the things that we value?'

This answer gets me some of the way, but often audiences are still sceptical. I get this. In today's age, it is not enough to make proclamations about what 'ought' to be done without providing some evidence to support the case. This moves me to give a second answer, but it is not a perfect answer. I actually don't want it to come across as a perfect answer, as anyone who tells you they have an accurate measure for character, without any limitations, is being economical with the truth. An accurate measure of character simply does not exist anywhere in the world. It is also not likely to in the near future.

My partial answer goes something like this: 'While we can't measure the whole of someone's character, we can measure some component parts of their virtues.'

If you think about it, the situation is not much different to maths. We never try to 'measure' someone's ability to do the whole of the maths curriculum. We break down maths into different topics and test these.

If you want to evaluate if your child is growing in character and cyber-wisdom, look out for these signs:[2]

- Do your children increasingly notice situations online that require them to respond virtuously? For example, do they tell you when they have spotted cyber-bullying online involving one of their friends?

- Do your children increasingly use a language of character and cyber-wisdom? Do they appear to know and understand these terms? For example, do they talk about explicit virtues (in the positive or negative) when they are describing theirs and others' lives online?

- Do your children increasingly show the right virtue-relevant emotion when they describe situations that have happened to them online? For example, do they get angry when they have witnessed injustice online, and happy when they have witnessed kindness on social media?

- Do your children appear to be increasingly committed to virtues in their online actions? Are those becoming part of their identity? For example, do they describe themselves as someone who is trying to act with integrity in all their online interactions?

- Do your children seem to be making increasingly better decisions when online, especially when they are faced with online situations where virtues conflict or collide? For example, do they sometimes choose to be honest with you about one of their friends' negative online actions rather than be loyal to their friend?

- Finally, and most importantly, do you increasingly witness your children acting with virtues and wisdom in their daily online actions? They might not always do so, but do they seem to be learning from past experiences and striving to do the right thing in the right way when online? For example, do they tell you about times they have used social media to help, support and improve the lives of other people?

Most probably you won't see a linear improvement over time across these components. Sometimes your children will appear to be making more good decisions, and at other times they will appear to be falling back.

For each of these components, we can construct measures. Some are easier to construct and for some the measure will be more accurate than others. For example, we can 'test' students' knowledge and understanding of cyber-wisdom in a well-constructed pencil-and-paper test and we can design experiments to see if they can perceive situations that stand in need of a virtuous response. It is harder to construct accurate measures for virtue emotion, and I believe virtue action and practice can only really be measured through careful, longitudinal and intense observational studies.

This presents a problem for the character educationalist, as the ultimate aim of character education is virtue action and practice. We want our children to make better decisions online. We want them to show character and cyber-wisdom as a matter of course. Although I can't suggest an accurate measure, I can suggest something just as good: your own knowledge, experience and intuition. We know, I believe, when our children are, and are not, displaying particular virtues.

The components are not only helpful for measurements and

evaluation; they also provide some pointers about where to target character-education interventions. We can teach our children knowledge and understanding of cyber-wisdom, we can help them spot times in their lives that stand in need of a virtuous response, we can even help them to become better at reasoning with virtue. By targeting these components, we make it more likely that they will cultivate and hone the quality of cyber-wisdom.

Dialogue and discussion are at the heart of good character education

Dialogue and discussion are central to many of the activities outlined in the next chapter. Character education is not a one-way process, otherwise it is simply mindless conditioning. Good character education occurs when there is space and freedom for honest and sometimes challenging conversations, where everyone involved has a voice.

I use dilemmas a lot in my work with children as they are a great way to start discussions and get them debating and weighing up different courses of action. They are also useful when you want to discuss issues with your children in a way that is not too intrusive. Some children are more likely to open up when they don't feel they have to get personal.

Dialogue and discussion might be seen to stimulate moral reasoning, but they are also a chance for us to compare and weigh up different perspectives and viewpoints. Several writers in the field have foregrounded the importance of dialogue. For example, the cognitive development model proposed by Lawrence Kohlberg and most recently the Philosophy for Children (P4C) movement.[3] These, in some way or another, draw on what has been termed the Socratic method. The method provides a basis for critical thinking where the focus for the teacher and parent is to ask questions and not give the answers. Our role is to model the enquiring mind. It also demands that we have some structure in place that allows for full, frank discussion and learning.

When setting up a discussion with children (one or many) about their online lives, consider the following:

- Make sure your children share an understanding with you about what the Internet is. Are you talking about the whole of the Internet, or a particular game, app or social media website? What are the boundaries for the discussion?

- Make sure you share a language or at least some common terms that you can all use to discuss your experiences of living online. When terms or phrases are used by your children that you don't understand, ask them to explain them.

- Give your children some facts about how the Internet is changing their and others' lives so that their thoughts and opinions are based on evidence where it is available. Recent surveys, news articles and similar data make great conversation starters.

- If you are running a dialogue with a group of children, you may need to be an active facilitator to ensure that all of those who want to contribute get a chance to speak.

- Don't think the aim of the discussion is always to arrive at a shared point of view; be comfortable with the fact that your children might leave the discussion thinking differently from you.

- Encourage children to think critically. This means challenge their own and others' points of view.

- Ensure everyone is listening. They don't have to agree with what others are saying, but they should have at least properly heard, thought about and taken on board alternative opinions.

- It is not your role to bring your own opinion in (although the situation might demand it); your main role is to start the discussion, facilitate it, and summarise key points and areas of contention.

If you want to bring some structure to the discussion, you could use the following open question prompts:

Do you all know what we are talking about? For example, if you were discussing an incident of cyber-bullying, you might provide a definition of cyber-bullying and some statistics about it.

Do you think the situation is immoral? Here you are trying to get a group opinion on what they think is and is not acceptable behaviour and why. During this process you should be able to arrive at an understanding about what the group thinks is and is not acceptable online behaviour.

What demands does this situation place on your own and others' character? Here you are asking the children to identify the character-related issues of the situation. For example, what is it about cyber-bullying that people do not like? Where are the boundaries between banter and bullying? You might need to explain that not all situations are solvable – sometimes we have to settle for answers that are more or less right.

What can you or others do about it? This would be the final stage of a discussion that moves towards action. At this point, possible courses of action can be suggested and discussed.

CHAPTER 18: KEY MESSAGES

- Character education should not be indoctrinating – it is about helping children to become critically aware, autonomous thinkers and doers.

- Character can be caught, taught and sought. Character is mostly caught by growing up in certain environments. You can also adopt explicit approaches to 'teaching' character. Ultimately, we want children to seek out opportunities to show character and cyber-wisdom through their own volition.

- Don't get too hung up on trying to measure your children's character growth, as this is very hard to do in practice. There are some components of virtue that you can try to observe growth in over time.

- Parents and teachers seeking to educate for character and cyber-wisdom have to play a number of roles, including working together to encourage children to talk about their lives online. Dialogue and discussion are at the heart of good character education.

19

Activities to Cultivate Cyber-wisdom

There is no magic bullet to 'teach' cyber-wisdom. There is no single activity or set of activities that are guaranteed to make children possess the quality. The activities described in this concluding chapter should help you hone cyber-wisdom in your children, but they will not *make* them cyber-wise.

The word 'hone' is important to focus on. To hone is to suggest that children already possess some wisdom and our job is to deepen and sharpen this quality. To deepen is to recognise that as children get older, the online moral dilemmas and issues they face become more complex and demand greater strength of character. To sharpen is to help our children to make increasingly better decisions as they grow older and gain autonomy.

To hone is not to teach; it is to shape, form, enhance and refine our children – starting with who they are.

The activities described below can be adopted and delivered by teachers and parents as they are described. Most, however, will need some adaptation. You know your children best – your knowledge of them is the starting point for adapting the activities. Taken as a whole, the activities might be viewed as a form of spiral curriculum. You can come back to each of them over time, to go over the same ideas, concepts and knowledge. Each time you return to them, the activities will be viewed differently, reflecting the fact that our children's experiences and understanding of their cyber-worlds are likely to change.

We all develop our characters over time. We develop them by facing similar situations and challenges, and learning how to respond appropriately. In this sense the activities are neither static nor designed for a particular age group. Most are suitable, with some adaptation, for children between the ages of ten and sixteen.

To bring some coherence to the educational activities, I have organised them around five stages that are each designed to contribute to our children becoming cyber-wise. The five stages are:

The five stages of cyber-wisdom

1. Inspiring: If children are to develop cyber-wisdom, we have to start by capturing their imagination. When we inspire children, we show them what is possible. I have explained previously how you can construct and use exemplars in educational activities as a form of inspiration. Having been inspired, we need children to aspire to be cyber-wise. I suggest an activity that encourages children to develop this aspiration by designing a brave new online world – a world that they would like to live in.

2. Knowing and Understanding: We need to provide children with a language with which they can think and talk about their cyber-lives. They need to develop a form of cyber-wisdom literacy. The best way to cultivate this language is through conversation. Through the possession of this language, they are in a better position to know and understand more about the moral issues in their cyber-worlds. It's one thing to know about the cyber-world and cyber-wisdom, but it's another to really understand these concepts.

3. Empowering: Children need to identify how cyber-technologies influence their lives and recognise that they have control over them. I describe an activity that will help children think about what they *need* and what they *want* cyber-technologies for. Through this process they will understand how to self-regulate their use of the Internet.

4. Reasoning: To be cyber-wise is to be able to reason through various courses of action and decide which is the best one to take. I explain how you can use ethical dilemmas as a form of character education. The activities I describe will encourage children to think through the online ethical dilemmas they face and how doing so helps them to make wiser, character-based judgements.

5. Acting and reflecting: Cyber-wisdom is about applied cognition: thinking and then doing. By reflecting on their actions, children learn. I describe an activity that will encourage children to put the pieces together and test out their cyber-wisdom in real life.

NOTE: Most of the educational activities are designed to work equally well in the home or at school. In the activities, children/students are mostly referred to as 'young people' to acknowledge that the activities are designed for ten- to sixteen-year-olds and might be led by teachers or parents.

A virtuous circle

It is possible to think of the five stages as an evolving virtuous circle. We start by trying to inspire young people to aspire to be cyber-wise. We then need to give them the tools and experiences to help them cultivate this quality in themselves – to know, to understand, to feel empowered, and to be able to reason independently. These qualities lead to action and practice, which should then be reflected upon.

Having reflected and revised their actions after positive or negative online experiences, young people might then seek out further experiences to build on their emerging cyber-wisdom. In this sense, the five stages can be seen as a virtuous circle of growth towards enhanced cyber-wisdom. It would be possible to structure a curriculum using these five stages, drawing on some or all of the suggested activities.

The activities I describe also act as a menu. You can choose to pick any of the seven activities and run them independently. For example, you might decide your children or students need help thinking through the ethical dilemmas they face online and choose to run the reasoning activity. You could also make up or adapt your own activities that link to one or more of the five areas.

It is, however, important to stress that what works with one of your children might not work with your other children. This is to say that there is no universal blueprint for character education. Your judgement is paramount; you need to use your own skills, experience and wisdom to judge how best to carry out the activities to gain the intended results. This will require you to conduct your own micro-action research projects, testing different approaches and evaluating what works and what does not work. Then, after you have revised them, try again.

Inspiring

If we are to educate young people to help them hone the quality of their cyber-wisdom, they first must be inspired. To be inspired is to see what is possible. It is to open up the imagination. A good way to inspire young people is by introducing them to role models and exemplars – a regular theme in this book.

Inspiration should lead to aspiration. To aspire is to actively seek out opportunities to develop the THRIVE qualities and to live by them when online. Aspiration, we should remember, does not always translate to accomplishment. It is, however, a necessary first step. To aspire is to identify with a particular way of life and to be motivated to try to obtain it. Activity 1 encourages children to think about what they aspire to for their cyber-worlds.

Activity 1: Brave New Online World

The Brave New Online World activity encourages young people to look at their cyber-world from a distance as well as from close up. The activity is designed to encourage young people to imagine the type of cyber-world they would like to live in and debate what qualities the individuals who live there should possess. It is about turning inspiration into aspiration.

The Brave New Online World activity is best carried out with young people working in small groups, but could be adapted into an activity a parent and child could work through together. The activity has six steps:

Step one
Introduce the idea of a brave new online world by reading out this passage from Shakespeare's *The Tempest*.

> O wonder!
> How many goodly creatures are there here!
> How beauteous mankind is! O brave new world,
> That has such people in't.
> — *William Shakespeare, The Tempest, Act V, Scene I*

This passage calls on us all to wonder what a brave new world that has goodly and beauteous people in it would look like. Explain to the young people that they enter a brave new world when they get their first smartphone or go online alone for the first time. Ask them to think back to how they were feeling when they first got a phone; did they know what type of world they would be entering? Some of them might rightly have been fearful, some might have heard stories about the dangers that lurk out there, others might have been excited. The point is to get the young people to understand that Internet access is the key to a new world, bringing with it new possibilities, opportunities, challenges and risks.

Older children might also be interested in thinking about Aldous Huxley's *Brave New World*. This book describes a dystopia where people end up wanting progress, comfort and entertainment so much that they eventually give up their freedom and their ability to think for themselves – in effect, they give up their virtue. Older children could think about the advantages and disadvantages of technologies in these terms.

Step two

Ask the young people, working on their own, to write down all the hopes they have for their lives online in the brave new world. These might be 'to make lots of friends', or 'to make a difference to others', or 'to find out new things'.

After they have made a list of hopes, ask them to write down all the fears they have about living in the cyber-world. These might be 'getting bullied' or 'not trusting who I talk to online'. In my experience, young people tend to have more fears than hopes. This might initiate a discussion on why this is the case.

Step three

Once the young people have written down their lists of hopes and fears, ask them to share some of them with the wider group. As they do so, keep a group list of the top hopes and fears on a piece of flip-chart paper.

Step four

Now ask the groups of young people to imagine that their hopes are realised and fears of living in their brave new world reduced. You should prompt the students to think about this with the following questions:

- What do they want their brave new cyber-worlds to look like?

- Who lives there?

- What can they do there?

- What can't they do there?

- What do they hope others can't do there?

- What do they hope others can do there?

- Why would they want to 'live' there?

Step five

Once they have created their world, ask the young people to list all the things they can do to make their imagined brave new world a reality. Ask them to put a star next to all the actions they believe to be in their power. They might think some of the items on their list primarily rely on the actions of other people, such as policy makers or those who run the Big Tech companies. Encourage them to also make a list of actions they could take that would influence policy makers or tech companies and the other gatekeepers that have the power to make their online world better.

Step six

Finish the activity by asking the young people to present to the rest of the group their ideas for their brave new cyber-world and what they can do to make their ideas a reality – focusing on their aspirations. Ask the rest of the group to state what they found inspiring about each of the presentations.

Knowing and understanding

It is important our children don't just know about how cyber-technologies work (for example, how to code), but also learn about how these technologies affect their and others' lives. We need them to become mini moral philosophers and ask ethical questions as well as try to answer them.

This means we must help young people develop a language and understanding of concepts that they can use to critically and, over time, autonomously evaluate how technology and the Internet impacts their lives. The possession of this language will help them address big questions like:

- How does my smartphone improve my life?

- How does my smartphone make my life harder?

- Am I over-reliant on technology?

- What ethical dilemmas does living with digital technologies raise for me and other people?

- Can I trust what I see online?

Using these questions, together with others you come up with, as a basis for conversations with young people is a great way to develop what might be called cyber-literacy. Activity 2 focuses on this.

Activity 2: Developing cyber-literacy

We have to get young people talking. This is how they develop language when they are young and this is how they expand it as they grow up. Developing cyber-literacy is no different from developing specialist language that might be associated with science, films or sport. In order to converse on these topics, we have to know certain words, but more importantly we have to know what they mean. Through talking, we can give young people this language and also help them better understand the worlds they live in. Once they have a language, young people will feel empowered to discuss and debate. They will develop the critical capacities and confidence to question what they are told and to make sense of it in their own terms.

The great thing about talking with young people is that it can be done at almost any time – it does not have to be a planned activity that we force on our children. We can talk to them over a meal, before they go to bed, on a long car journey, while playing a computer game with them. The important thing is to get the timing right. Sometimes my children just do not want to talk, and at other times they will happily discuss an issue for ages, asking expansive questions that take us in new directions. The key point is to try to help young people to talk about their cyber-lives – we have to create an atmosphere and environment that makes them want to do so. My children tell me that direct questions about their use of the phone sometimes feels accusatory and that open questions that start conversations are often more likely to have the desired effect. Another tactic I use is to sit with my daughter and ask her to talk me through one of her WhatsApp conversations – she leads the conversation. In the questions I ask and the language I use, she is learning a new vocabulary and so am I.

Below is a list of conversation starters that have been adapted from the Safer Internet Day[1] educational materials. I am sure you can think of many more.

- What do you like most about the Internet and why?

- What's your favourite game/app/site and why?

- How does going online make you feel?

- How does the Internet/technology make your life better?

- What could you do if being online is making you feel worse rather than better?

- What is different about talking online to someone compared to talking face to face? Is there anything that is the same?

- Can people say/do whatever they want online? Why/why not?

- Do you know where to go for help, where to find safety advice and how to use safety tools on your favourite apps and games?

- What is okay to share online? What is not okay to share online? Why?

- What could you do if you saw a friend online needed some help or support?

- How do you stay safe online? What tips do you have and where did you learn them?

- Help me! Can you show me how to do something better or safer online?

I particularly like the last one, as it requires a shift in power. It places young people as the 'experts' and we are asking them to teach or show us something. This will empower our children and demands they take some responsibility. It can also make the conversations between young people and adults more fulfilling and perhaps less threatening. If we can talk on the same level as young people, we will all improve our cyber-literacy as well as our knowledge and understanding about how cyber-technologies are affecting all of our lives.

Empowering

If we are to support young people to use the Internet wisely, we need to get them to think about how their identity is shaped by technology. We need them to consider these two questions:

1. What 'power' does the technology hold over them?

2. What 'power' do they hold over the technology?

Answering these questions will help young people think about how their identity shapes the technologies they use. If we can help them to understand that they are in control not only of what cyber-technologies they use, but also of what they are used for, they will see why character is so important. The aim is that, through such an investigation, young people will realise that they have the power to shape their and others' futures.

Activity 3: What do we need and what do we want?

This activity has two stages and starts by encouraging young people to identify who they think is in charge: technology or humans. In stage two, young people are required to think about when cyber-technologies are being used for the right or wrong reasons. The overall aim of the two stages is to help them identify when they and others are using cyber-technologies to help the world flourish and when this is not the case.

Step one: Our technology needs and wants

The aim of the first stage of the activity is for young people to identify what cyber-software (apps, games, social media, etc.) they 'have' to use and what cyber-software they use out of choice because they want to. Through discussion and dialogue about their technology needs and wants, the hope is that young people start to understand that much of their technology use is their choice – they understand that they have control over what they use and when.

Start by asking the young people (individually or in a group) to list all the cyber-software applications they have used in the last few weeks. This will probably include things like Facebook, online libraries, email, etc. Once they have made a list, ask them to categorise each item on their list by:

1.   putting an 'N' for need next to all the software they believe they absolutely have to use;

2.   putting a 'W' for want next to the software they use because they want to – the applications they choose to use.

Explain that they are in control of the software they have placed in the 'wants' category – but do they think this is the case? If not, ask them why? Then ask them to think about the software they have placed in their 'needs' category. Do they really need to use it? What will happen if they choose not to use it? Do they have any control over its use, such as how it is used and what it is used for?

At the end of the activity, ask the young people to sum up how they now think about their cyber-technology use. Has the activity made them think differently? Guide them into understanding that they have some control and that, much of the time, they are reacting to the release of new games or social media sites. If the young people start to believe they are mostly in control, they will also start to see that it is their character-based decisions that determine what software enhances their own and other people's lives.

Step two: How we use technologies

The aim of the second stage is for young people to reflect on how they use cyber-technologies. This builds on the first stage, as how they use technologies is shaped by and also shapes their identity. Start this step by giving the young people the following statements, each written on a separate card:

- I feel I am in charge of how I use the Internet.

- I can't stop using the Internet.

- The Internet is helping me to be a better friend.

- I have used the Internet to help others.

- The Internet can be the stimulus for great conversations.

- I wish I was not on social media.

- I wish I was not on social media as much as I am currently.

- I am a different person online compared to when I am offline.

- I only use some apps online because my friends do.

- I have changed my behaviour because of something that happened online.

- Sometimes technologies make me feel out of control.

Then ask the young people to plot each of the cards on one of the following types of scale.

- Plotting each statement on a piece of paper numbered from -10 (totally disagree) to +10 (totally agree).

- Using your hand – stretch your hand up (totally agree), or touch the ground (totally disagree), or somewhere in between.

- Moving around the room – one side of the room signifies totally agree and another totally disagree – the young people move around, depending on how they feel, from statement to statement.

Each of these statements is designed to help children think about how they use the Internet and the associated cyber-hardware and software. As they plot the statements on the scale, ask them to explain the reasons behind their judgements.

When they have completed the activity, ask them which statement worries them the most and why.

Reasoning

As has been explained throughout this book, good character is often about making good judgements. The idea is that the more experience we have, the better judgements we make. We need to develop and hone young people's ability to reason well if they are to improve their actions.

There is no better way of honing reason than in the heat of the moment: in a real-life situation. However, we can also help young people think about what decisions they might make by giving them hypothetical dilemmas embedded into structured educational activities. There is no guarantee young people will actually make the 'right' decision should they actually face the dilemma, but they are more likely to do so if they have given time and thought to it in advance. Ethical dilemmas are a test of character; they are also an important vehicle for character education.

Activity 4: Digital dilemmas

The aim of this activity is to support young people to make wiser choices in their online lives. It should help young people to think through what they might do when faced with hypothetical, yet realistic, dilemmas. To do so can be a good training ground for the 'real' world. Repeated exposure to dilemmas in an educational context can be seen as a form of advanced habituation where students are gradually brought to more critical discernment through the practice of cyber-wisdom.

The key here is to use the dilemmas to stimulate critical reflection. The featured dilemmas are all based on real-life examples. They can be used to stimulate discussion and debate. A good dilemma does not come with an obvious answer or contain a straightforward moral message – otherwise it is not a dilemma. However, over time we develop the ability to make better decisions and get more judgements 'right'. Using dilemmas in a taught character programme should help young people develop this quality more quickly.

Virtue perception and reasoning

At the heart of this activity are ten moral dilemmas, developed in collaboration with eleven- to fourteen-year-olds I have worked with. They are dilemmas that young people might face in their daily lives and relate to concerns such as cyber-bullying, plagiarism, piracy and extremism. Before young people can start to think about what they might do about these, they have to notice when they are faced with a dilemma that demands a moral response. To notice is to perceive and to perceive is often a trigger to pause and to think. Exposure to dilemmas, through the taught programme, helps our children to initially notice and then progress towards resolving conflicting moral demands. The activity therefore seeks to educate two components of virtue: perception and reasoning.

I use the dilemmas below in a taught programme I deliver in secondary schools called Making Wiser Choices Online.[2] In my work with schools and children I want to know if, after the programme, the young people who participate are better equipped to notice when they are in an online situation that demands a virtuous response. I conducted a study and found that the children who were exposed to the dilemmas in a taught programme had higher virtue reasoning and perception scores than those who had not. Interestingly, girls scored better than boys.

How to use the dilemmas?

All ten of the dilemmas listed below contain a clash of virtues. This is what makes them complex, as there are no straightforward or necessarily 'right' answers. This is also what makes them truer to the types of dilemmas we all face in real life.

There are a number of ways we can use the dilemmas as part of a more or less formal educational programme. Here are some suggestions. Home-based activities:

- Ask your child to sort the dilemmas into those they think are the easiest to address and those they think are the hardest, and ask them to explain why.

- Talk through some of the dilemmas with your child and ask them to explain if anything similar has happened to them or one of their friends. Work with your child to come up with an appropriate response to each of the dilemmas.

- Read through the dilemmas one at a time. For each, ask your child to identify which virtues are in opposition and to explain why each of these virtues is important. Finally, ask them to decide which one of the virtues they think is the most important in this situation, and to explain their answer.

School-based activities:

- Place the dilemmas in a hat and ask a group of young people to pick them out one at a time. Ask them to read out to the group the dilemma they picked and then discuss and decide together what they would do and give an explanation why.

- Ask the young people to construct a role-play of one of the dilemmas and show it to the rest of the group. The group then has to decide what the dilemma is and what they would do about it.

- Having read through the dilemmas, ask the young people to make a short film that gives the details of a similar dilemma that relates to their life. Show all the films at a screening and debate the central dilemmas depicted in each.

The dilemmas
Dilemma 1: Anna's unkind messages
Anna is very loyal to her best friend Rachel. However, Anna realises that Rachel has been sending bullying messages over the Internet to another girl at school. Anna does not really like the other girl, but she also thinks the messages that Rachel has been sending are not kind. One day at

school, Anna's teacher asks her if she knows who has been sending the nasty messages. What should Anna do?

Dilemma 2: Bashra loves films

Bashra is thirteen years old and loves films. She feels as though everyone at her school has recently been to the cinema to watch the sequel to one of her favourites. She really wants to see it too, but knows that her parents won't take her because it has a fifteen certificate. She looks the film up online and notices she can download it onto her computer in her bedroom. What should Bashra do?

Dilemma 3: James's joke

James is always on his favourite social networking site. He regularly posts and replies to messages to his friends. He decides to set up an anonymous account and sends nasty messages to one of his friends as a joke. He does this for several days and thinks it is very funny. However, one day he notices his friend is looking upset at school. What should he do?

Dilemma 4: Mohammed on Twitter

Mohammed has set up a new Twitter account. He is on it all the time and constantly trying to connect with new people to get more followers so that he can promote his fundraising page for a charity he is running an event for. Mohammed realises that when he posts rude tweets to people, he gets more followers, even though he doesn't necessarily believe what he is saying. He assumes that the more followers he gets, the more money he will earn for the charity. What should Mohammed do?

Dilemma 5: Smoking Jenny

For the first time ever, at a friend's party, Jenny had a cigarette. She did not want to, but all her friends were smoking. She felt ill afterwards and was sick. Jenny did not realise that her friend had taken photos on her phone of her smoking and being ill afterwards, and had posted the pictures to her social networking page. When she woke up the next morning, she found the pictures had been shared with many students at her school. What should Jenny do?

Dilemma 6: Paul's worries

Paul is being bullied online. The first time it happened, he ignored it. However, he has received nasty messages several times and these have made him both angry and upset. He thinks he knows who is sending them, and wants to get revenge, but he does not know how. What should Paul do?

Dilemma 7: Rosie and the unknown 'friend'

Rosie shares everything with her best friend Jo. Rosie has been chatting to a boy in a social media chatroom and has planned to meet him next week. She has lied about her age and has told the boy she is sixteen, when she is actually fourteen. Jo is worried about what will happen when they meet up, as Rosie doesn't really know anything about this boy apart from his age and name. What should Jo do?

Dilemma 8: Chris becomes a member

Chris is browsing the Internet when an alert pops up. It looks exciting, so Chris clicks on it and it takes him to a website. Chris doesn't like the website and he finds some of the things on it quite offensive and disturbing. He tries to click off it, but, before he knows it, he has become a member of the website. Chris is really worried about this. What should he do?

Dilemma 9: Bill and extreme groups

Bill is having a hard time at school and at home. His best friend Jim is very worried about him and notices he has started to become withdrawn and is isolating himself from friends. Jim knows Bill has been visiting some very disturbing websites and that he has asked to join some very radical/extreme online groups. Bill doesn't know much about these groups, but feels he should join one as they say they understand what he is going through. Jim is worried about these groups and what they are doing to Bill. What should Jim do?

Dilemma 10: Sabir and the made-up story

Sabir is always on the Internet. He uses it for research all the time. One day he is on Wikipedia with his friend. His friend tells him that he likes to make up things about famous people and add these to their Wikipedia site. He thinks this is funny. However, Sabir is worried that this is misleading people around the world. He does not want to get his friend in trouble, but does not want misinformation on the website. What should Sabir do?

Acting and reflecting

The ultimate goal of all the activities described so far, in fact the objective of this whole book, is to make it more likely that young people will act with wisdom, character and virtue when they are online. We can't make them act in the way we want them to, nor should we. True character is virtuous behaviour that is undertaken autonomously. The activity suggested in this section is about helping our young people to become wise online cyber-citizens independently and not through coercion.

Activity 5: Cyber-wisdom journal

This activity is based on young people recording the times they are called on to show cyber-wisdom over the course of a week. It can be an intense activity that takes time and dedication, but it can also be extremely illuminating. It is an activity that young people are unlikely to carry out independently, and you will probably have to remind and support them to complete it. At its heart, the activity is a form of experiential learning.

The activity has three stages.

Stage 1: Understanding the purpose

Make sure the young people understand what cyber-wisdom is. Explain that it is needed every time they are called on to make a decision about a moral issue related to cyber-technologies. These can be very small or very large decisions. Give them some examples, such as:

- if they spot a friend bullying another on WhatsApp;

- if they discover one of their friends is cheating in their online homework;

- if they have to make a decision between helping cook dinner or playing an online game;

- if they see a friend reporting someone they know for bullying behaviour.

Once they understand what sort of online activities demand that they show cyber-wisdom, ask the young people to give you some of their own examples.

Stage 2: Keeping a journal

Ask the young people to keep a journal, like the one below, for one week (you might also want to keep your own journal at the same time). It requires them to record instances when they or someone they know have or have not shown cyber-wisdom at three points each day – in the morning, in the afternoon and in the evening. If they did not use cyber-technologies for any of these periods, they should leave the section blank. Explain that the instances don't have to be big and that almost every time they communicate with someone online, they are making a judgement or decision about what to say. The aim of the exercise is to put a microscope onto their cyber-lives for a week.

My cyber-wisdom journal

Day	Time	Summary of online activity: what was I doing and for how long?	An instance when I or someone else showed cyber-wisdom	An instance when I or someone I know did not show cyber-wisdom
Monday	Morning			
	Afternoon			
	Evening			
Tuesday	Morning			
	Afternoon			
	Evening			
Wednesday	Morning			
	Afternoon			
	Evening			
Thursday	Morning			
	Afternoon			
	Evening			
Friday	Morning			
	Afternoon			
	Evening			
Saturday	Morning			
	Afternoon			
	Evening			
Sunday	Morning			
	Afternoon			
	Evening			

Stage 3: Guided reflection

At the end of the week, ask the young people to reflect on what they have learnt from keeping the journal. If you also kept a diary, share your experiences and reflections. Structure the reflective discussion using the following questions:

- What surprised you about keeping the journal?

- What did not surprise you about keeping the journal?

- What activity made it most likely that you were not showing cyber-wisdom and why was this the case?

- What activity made it most likely that you did show cyber-wisdom and why was this the case?

- What will you do differently in the future having kept the journal?

- What have you learnt about yourself, others and online technologies from keeping the journal?

Make sure, as you run the guided reflection, that it:

- has a clear purpose: that young people understand the importance of reflection for personal growth;

- is progressive: each reflection should build on any that have gone before;

- is honest and positive: it should utilise a 'what went well' and 'even better if' approach.

There are different ways that parents and teachers can extend the reflection activity suggested above. These include:

- Different perspectives: take on board the reflections from friends, teachers, parents and others.

- Different audiences: reflecting individually, with friends, in a small or large group.

- Different modes: verbal, online, written, in a film, etc.

- Different timescales: reflection immediately after an online incident or after a month or year of a young person living online.

CHAPTER 19: KEY MESSAGES

- Just as there is no blueprint for character education, there is no magic bullet for teaching cyber-wisdom. Well-run, structured education activities will, however, make it more likely that children develop this quality.

- The activities I describe aim to:

  - **Inspire**, by imagining brave new cyber-worlds.

  - **Teach cyber-wisdom literacy**, by starting conversations that will develop a knowledge and understanding of why character and wisdom matter in the cyber-world.

  - **Empower**, by helping young people gain control over their use of cyber-technologies.

  - **Reason and be better prepared**, by thinking through online ethical dilemmas.

  - **Act with wisdom and reflect**, by learning through experience.

Summary of Part Four: Cultivating Character and Cyber-wisdom

Part Four describes practical strategies for cultivating cyber-wisdom within a character-education framework. Although there are an increasing number of books and resources available that focus on character education more generally, very few of them include specific educational support and advice that focuses on helping children and young people use the Internet more wisely. Drawing inspiration from well-known and well-tested character-education approaches, the advice in Part Four demonstrates how these might be adapted and directed to cultivate cyber-wisdom in children and young people.

Key areas of practical advice in Part Four include:

- An overview of the recent global interest in character education – why more people are taking it seriously and why you should too if you want your children to flourish online.

- How to make sure your character education is not indoctrinating or a form of mindless conditioning.

- How character is caught, taught, but ultimately should be sought. How we help children to independently desire and seek out opportunities to demonstrate cyber-wisdom under their own volition.

- How we can't seek to shape the whole of a person's character. Instead, we have to break character down into its building blocks – virtues – and then break the virtues down into their component parts.

- How parents and teachers can work together as character educators.

Part Four concludes by detailing activities designed to educate the five stages of becoming cyber-wise. The five stages are:

1. **Inspire** young people to live well in a cyber-world worth living in.

2. Building **knowledge** in young people to help them **understand** what character and cyber-wisdom are.

3. **Empower** young people so they can take back control of their cyber-worlds – putting them in the driving seat.

4. Developing skills of autonomous **reasoning** in young people – priming them to deal virtuously with online ethical dilemmas.

5. Providing opportunities for young people to learn through **reflecting** on their **practice** towards becoming cyber-wise.

Conclusion

I end this book where I started. My daughter has now had her mobile phone for a year. She is again using the phone in the room next door. I am no longer nervous. My initial nerves about giving her a phone have dissipated as I have observed how she has used the phone. It has not turned out to be the 'monster in the room' or even as much of a rite of passage as I thought it might be. In many ways the phone has improved her and our lives. She mainly uses it to make arrangements, and during the pandemic lockdown it allowed her to stay in touch with her friends when they were off school, which was important. The phone memory is full of pictures of our lives during the lockdown as well as of fun times she had with friends and us before it. I have observed her use the phone in a positive way when we were forced into home schooling – as a calculator, to look up facts, and to check in with her friends about something she was unsure on.

The phone has given her independence and, in some way, taken her away from us. I think this was going to happen anyway and I don't believe the phone has unduly speeded this process up. In some ways our children live in different worlds, and the affordances their laptops and phones give them mean they can interact with friends and other people in ways we could only dream about at their age. But, in many ways, things have not changed. I try to parent my children how I was parented. The challenges might be different, but my values and principles that guide what I expect and hope for my children are similar. I was brought up surrounded by a great deal of love, but also boundaries. Many of these boundaries related to expectations on behaviour. Be kind, be thoughtful, be determined, be honest and try to be courageous. The love meant I was more respectful and attentive to the boundaries. I hope that I have passed this on to my children. I have put in place boundaries and expectations for their use of the Internet, but I also hope they know I love them.

Having written this book, I have fulfilled a personal hope. My aim, as I stated at the start, was no longer to know what to *think*, but to know more about what to *do*. In researching for the book, I have read hundreds of publications and spoken to parents, teachers and colleagues. I think I have learnt most through observing my own parenting in practice. I have tried to consciously reflect on how well I apply the REACT model. I have been much more aware of what rules I put in place for my daughter's use of the Internet and when I should start to take these down. I have certainly become much more conscious about my own phone and Internet use, and the messages I unintentionally convey to my children when using these. I have a long way to go to get to the level of Gandhi as an exemplar, but I hope I'm a better role model than I was before I started the book. I regularly ask my daughter how she is finding living in the cyber-world, and try to be attentive to her changing moods and whether these might be connected to her interactions online. We have not had any serious incidents connected with her Internet use to date, but I do anticipate there will be some challenging episodes as she continues to grow up. Because of my job, I hope I have always been a character champion. However, it is one thing to write books and tell people in presentations what this involves, it is another to enact it in day-to-day life. You will have to ask my son and daughter how I am doing on this. Will my parenting, following the REACT model, ensure my daughter thrives online? Only time will tell, but I am confident she is more likely to than if I had not been as conscious in my parenting.

I hope this book has inspired you to be more conscious about how you parent in the digital age. In particular, I hope it has made you more aware of the fantastic opportunities the Internet offers our children and more aware of the risks of going online and why we must help our children navigate around them. I also hope it helps you understand why character and cyber-wisdom are essential if our children are to flourish in the future. As I have stressed throughout, this book was never intended to be a blueprint for parenting in the digital age. Instead, I hope through my explaining the theory, and providing practical advice, you are able to think about how you apply the components of the REACT model in your own homes, schools and communities.

My son will get his first phone in the next year. I have all of this to come again. I will have to apply each component of the model differently to reflect my son's character and personality traits. It's a challenge I am looking forward to.

Notes

Preface

[1] I have been the Director of Education at the Jubilee Centre for Character and Virtues at the University of Birmingham for the past nine years. In this post I have been privileged to work alongside some of the foremost experts in character and character education in the world. Much of the theory and practice described in this book is inspired by the work of my colleagues in the Jubilee Centre. See www.jubileecentre.ac.uk for more details.

[2] The etymology of the word 'deontology' (meaning the science of moral duty) is from the Greek *deon*, which means 'that which is binding or duty'. It was an idea first proposed by Immanuel Kant, the German philosopher born in 1724. Kant is still considered today one of the most central figures in modern philosophy.

[3] The word 'utilitarianism' is first thought to have been used in 1827 and is widely understood as a doctrine that believes the aim of all action should be the greatest happiness for the greatest number. In philosophy, utilitarianism and consequentialism are often used interchangeably. The moral theoretical approach was associated initially with the British philosopher, Jeremy Bentham, born in 1748. The philosophy of Bentham was built on by, and became more popular through, the work of John Stuart Mill.

[4] The research into whether people behave morally better or worse online is not clear. My own and other people's research have shown that features of the Internet, such as the possibility of acting anonymously and ease of access, make it more likely that people will

undertake immoral acts online that they would not undertake offline.

[5] Cyber-wisdom derives from the Aristotelian term *phronesis*, which is widely translated today as 'practical wisdom'.

[6] It is part of the Personal Development judgement. Before 2019, Behaviour and Personal Development were combined in the same judgement, and character was not mentioned in the Ofsted framework.

[7] Southgate talks about the character of his players a lot in interviews. Here are two examples: 'We play with character and I love that about them' (quoted in the *Telegraph*, 3 June 2018) and 'The questions around us principally come down to character; the essential ability to withstand events that go against you' (quoted in the *Independent*, 11 June 2017).

[8] Quoted in *The Times*, Saturday 11 January 2020.

[9] See a paper published in 2020 by Wee and de Vauvert for a good overview of the evidence. The paper can be accessed here: https://www.jubileecentre.ac.uk/1609/papers/insight-series.

[10] See, for example, the article by Matthew Syed in the *Sunday Times* on 7 June 2020.

[11] Martin Luther King Jr wrote these words in an article entitled 'The Purpose of Education', published in 1947.

Chapter 1: Taking Back Control of Our Cyber-worlds
[1] It is well known that many of these features are 'designed' by tech companies to hold our attention in order to gain greater revenue. Although 'Internet addiction' is problematic, this is not the central focus of this book. This book is less about how much our children use their Internet-connected devices and more about what they use them for. Do they use them for good or not-so-good ends?

[2] The 'Don't be evil' motto was almost entirely removed from Google's code of conduct when the company changed its name to Alphabet in 2015.

[3] As reported in the *Telegraph*, 13 November 2019.

[4] The Big Tech industry is being criticised increasingly for causing social harms. For example, former Google employee Tristram Harris now runs the Centre for Humane Technology. He is leading a group of activists who are campaigning for ethical design to be built into digital technologies. He might argue that we need people of character to develop the technologies of the future.

Chapter 2: Parenting in the Cyber-age

[1] In the 1940s, the term 'cyber' came back into more common parlance through the work of Norbert Wiener, who wrote a book called *Cybernetics*. More recently, the term 'cyber' has become synonymous with the term 'cybernetic' and has been used to describe the integration of humans and technology. Today, it is a field in its own right, which in its broadest sense is a multi-disciplinary study of how machines and humans communicate with each other.

[2] As reported in this BBC story: https://www.bbc.co.uk/news/education-51296197.

[3] The taught, caught and sought classification comes from the Jubilee Centre Framework for Character Education – see https://www.jubileecentre.ac.uk/userfiles/jubileecentre/pdf/character-education/Framework%20for%20Character%20Education.pdf.

Chapter 3: From Online Risks to Online Opportunities

[1] Katz, J. (1997), *Virtuous Reality: How America Surrendered Discussion of Moral Values to Opportunists, Nitwits and Blockheads*. New York: Random House.

[2] Tapscott, D. (1998), *Growing Up Digital*. New York: McGraw-Hill.

[3] Shapiro, J. (2018), *The New Childhood*. New York: Little Brown Spark.

[4] As reported in *The Conversation* news story: https://theconversation.com/is-social-media-messing-with-childrens-morals-62579.

[5] 'Status of mind: Social media and young people's mental health and wellbeing' (2017) can be downloaded from here: https://www.rsph.org.uk/uploads/assets/uploaded/d125b27c-0b62-41c5-a2c0155a8887cd01.pdf.

[6] 'Initial findings from the Millennium Cohort Study Age 14 Sweep' (2017) can be downloaded from here: https://cls.ucl.ac.uk/cls_research/initial-findings-from-the-millennium-cohort-study-age-14-survey/.

[7] 'United Kingdom Chief Medical Officers' commentary on "Screen-based activities and children and young people's mental health and psychosocial wellbeing: A systematic map of reviews"' (2019) can be downloaded from here: https://assets.publishing.service.gov.uk/government/uploads/system/uploads/attachment_data/file/777026/UK_CMO_commentary_on_screentime_and_social_media_map_of_reviews.pdf.

[8] House of Commons Science and Technology Committee (2019), 'Impact of social media and screen time on young people's health', can be downloaded from here: https://publications.parliament.uk/pa/cm201719/cmselect/cmsctech/822/822.pdf.

[9] John, A., et al. (2018), 'Self-harm, suicidal behaviours, and cyberbullying in children and young people: Systematic review'. *Journal of Medical Internet Research*, 20(4).

[10] Statistics from National Crime Prevention Council report (2007) can be downloaded from here: https://www.ncpc.org/wp-content/uploads/2017/11/NCPC_Cyberbullying-WhatIsIt.pdf.

[11] 'ChildLine online issues report 2012–13' can be downloaded from here: https://www.thechildrensmediafoundation.org/wp-content/uploads/2014/02/Childline-online-issues-2012-13-summary.pdf.

[12] 'Cyberbullying: An analysis of data from the health behaviour in school-aged children (HBSC) survey for England (2014)' can be downloaded from here: https://assets.publishing.service.gov.uk/government/uploads/system/uploads/attachment_data/file/621070/Health_behaviour_in_school_age_children_cyberbullying.pdf.

[13] Carr, N. (2011), *The Shallows: What the Internet is Doing to our Brains*. New York: W.W. Norton and Company.

[14] Greenfield, S. (2014), *Mind Change: How Digital Technologies are Leaving Their Mark on Our Brains*. Ebury Digital.

[15] Sanders, M. and Hume, S. (2019), *Social Butterflies: Reclaiming the Positive Power of Social Networks*. London: Michael O'Mara Books.

[16] Clough, D. (2002), *Unweaving the Web: Beginning to Think Theologically about the Internet*. Cambridge: Grove Books Limited.

[17] Sonia Livingstone is the Professor of Social Psychology in the Department of Media and Communications at the London School of Economics (LSE).

[18] Livingstone, S. (2009), *Children and the Internet*. Cambridge: Polity Press, p. 30.

Chapter 4: From Digital Natives to Cyber-citizens

[1] Prensky, M. (2001), Do they really think different? *On the Horizon*, 9(5), pp.1–6.

[2] The letter is said to be written by Haim Ginott, a headteacher at a private school. He sent letters to all his teachers on the first day of term.

[3] Aristotle also suggested there was a third type of knowledge – *episteme*, which is science or theoretical knowledge.

[4] The open letter was published on 12 March 2019 and can be found on the Web Foundation website here: https://webfoundation.org/2019/03/web-birthday-30/.

[5] 'Children and parents: Media use and attitudes report 2018' can be downloaded from here: https://www.ofcom.org.uk/__data/assets/pdf_file/0024/134907/children-and-parents-media-use-and-attitudes-2018.pdf.

Chapter 5: Introducing the REACT and THRIVE Models

[1] Orben, A. and Przybylski, A. (2019), 'The association between adolescent well-being and digital technology use'. *Nature Human Behaviour*, 3(2), pp. 173–82.

[2] The Royal College of Paediatrics and Child Health report on screen-time (2019) can be downloaded from: https://www.rcpch.ac.uk/news-events/news/new-screen-time-research-published-rcpch-responds.

Chapter 7: Be a Ground-rule-maker

[1] Taken from the Facebook Policy statement found at: https://www.facebook.com/help/157793540954833 (emphasis added).

[2] See www.parentzone.org.uk/home.

3 See www.commonsensemedia.org/.

4 Mullan, M. and Chatzitheochari, S. (2019), 'Changing times together? A time–diary analysis of family time in the digital age in the United Kingdom'. *Journal of Marriage and Family*, 81(4), pp. 795–811.

5 Turkle, S. (2013), *Alone Together*. New York: Basic Books.

6 The OfCom communications market report (2018) can be downloaded from: https://www.ofcom.org.uk/research-and-data/multi-sector-research/cmr/cmr-2018.

7 Shapiro, J. (2019), *The New Childhood*. New York: Little Brown Spark.

8 As reported in this BBC story: https://www.bbc.co.uk/news/education-51296197.

9 See https://ourpact.com/.

10 Kagge, E. (2017), *Silence: In the Age of Noise*. New York: Penguin.

11 See: https://www.commonsensemedia.org/.

12 John Suler wrote several extremely well-known papers. Most of his key theories can be found in Suler, J. (2004), 'The online disinhibition effect'. *Cyberpsychology & Behaviour*, 3, pp. 151–60.

Chapter 8: Be an Exemplar
1 Plomin, R. (2018), *Blueprint: How DNA Makes Us Who We Are*. London: Penguin.

2 Harrison, T., Taylor, E. and Moller, F. (2018), 'A habit of service: The factors that sustain service in young people'. Jubilee Centre for Character

and Virtues, University of Birmingham, can be downloaded from: https://www.jubileecentre.ac.uk/userfiles/jubileecentre/pdf/Research %20Reports/A_Habit_of_Service.pdf.

[3] Zagzebski, L. (2019), *Exemplarist Moral Theory*. New York, Oxford University Press.

Chapter 9: Be an Advisor

[1] Brooks, D. (2019), *The Second Mountain: The Quest for a Moral Life.* New York: Random House.

[2] Dewey, J. (2011), *Democracy and Education*. Milton Keynes: Simon and Brown.

[3] Juvonen, J. and Gross, E. F. (2008), 'Extending the school grounds: Bullying experiences in cyberspace'. *Journal of School Health*, 78(9), pp. 496–505.

[4] Goodyear, V. and Armour, K. (2018), *Social Media, Young People, and Health*. London: Routledge.

Chapter 10: Be a Character Champion

[1] J. C. Watts spoke these words at the 1996 GOP National Convention.

[2] See, for example, Kristján Kristjánsson's excellent 2015 book *Aristotelian Character Education*. London: Routledge.

[3] Annas, J. (2011), *Intelligent Virtue*. Oxford: Oxford University Press.

[4] Well-known proponents of the situationist arguments include John Doris – see his 2002 book *Lack of Character: Personality and Moral Behavior*. New York: Cambridge University Press.

[5] See, for example, Doris, J., ibid.

[6] Blasi, A. (1980), 'Bridging moral cognition and moral action: A critical review of the literature'. *Psychological Bulletin*, 88(1), pp. 1–45.

[7] Aristotle called this the 'golden' mean of the virtue.

[8] Quotation from Aristotle, translated by Thomson, A. (1976), in *Ethics*. Middlesex: Penguin, pp. 91, 92.

Chapter 11: Be Thoughtful

[1] See https://demos.co.uk/project/service-generation/.

[2] See https://www.demos.co.uk/files/Generation_Citizen_-_web.pdf?1392764120.

[3] See https://www.iwill.org.uk.

[4] See http://www.helpfromhome.org/.

[5] See https://www.psychologytoday.com/gb/blog/the-squeaky-wheel/201307/10-surprising-facts-about-rejection.

[6] Quoted in *The Times*, 20 February 2020; see https://www.thetimes.co.uk/article/dont-blame-social-media-its-us-thats-the-problem-qzwm3s22p.

[7] See https://www.bbc.co.uk/cbbc/findoutmore/own-it-app.

Chapter 12: Be Human

[1] Turkle, S. (2013), *Alone Together*. New York: Basic Books.

[2] Firth, J., Torous, J., Stubbs, B., Steiner, G., Smith, L., Alvarez–Jimenez, M., Gleeson, J., Vancampfort, D., Armitage, C. and Sarris, J. (2019), 'The "online brain": How the Internet may be changing our cognition'. *World Psychiatry*, 18(2), p. 119.

[3] See, for example, Neil Selwyn (2019), *Should Robots Replace Teachers?* Cambridge: Polity.

[4] Baldwin, R. (2019), *The Globotics Upheaval: Globalisation, Robotics and the Future of Work*. Oxford: Oxford University Press.

[5] As reported in a *Times* article on Thursday 27 January 2020; see https://www.thetimes.co.uk/article/google-boss-sundar-pichai-artificial-intelligence-will-do-more-for-humanity-than-fire-0c9fp2wp2.

Chapter 13: Be ReasonABLE

[1] James, C. (2014), *Disconnected: Youth, New Media and the Ethics Gap*. London: MIT Press.

[2] See the report here: https://demosuk.wpengine.com/wp-content/uploads/2017/09/DEMJ5689-The-moral-Web-ethics-and-behaviour-on-social-media-170908-WEB-3.pdf.

Chapter 14: Have Integrity

[1] As reported in the *New York Times Magazine* on 12 February 2015; see https://www.nytimes.com/2015/02/15/magazine/how-one-stupid-tweet-ruined-justine-saccos-life.html.

[2] Gardner, H. and Davis, K. (2013), *The app generation: How today's youth navigate identity, intimacy, and imagination in a digital world*. New Haven: Yale University Press.

[3] Goffman, E. (1959), *The Presentation of Self in Everyday Life*. Garden City, NY: Doubleday.

[4] See https://fstoppers.com/mobile/68-percent-adults-edit-their-selfies-sharing-them-anyone-95417.

Chapter 15: Be an Exemplar

[1] See https://www.jubileecentre.ac.uk/userfiles/jubileecentre/pdf/character-education/Framework%20for%20Character%20Education.pdf.

[2] Brooks, D. (2015), *The Road to Character*. London, Penguin.

[3] Suler, J. (2004), 'The online disinhibition effect'. *Cyberpsychology & Behaviour*, 3, pp. 151–60.

[4] See, for example, Mishnan, F., Cook, C., Gadalla, T., Daciuk, J. and Solomon, S. (2010), 'Cyber-bullying behaviors among middle and high school students'. *The American Journal of Orthopsychiatry*, 80(3), pp. 362–74.

Chapter 17: Cultivating Cyber-wisdom through Character Education

[1] Safer Internet Day is run by the UK Safer Internet Centre, which is a partnership of three organisations: Childnet International, Internet Watch Foundation and SWGfL, with the mission to promote the safe and responsible use of technology for young people. See https://www.saferinternet.org.uk/.

[2] See an overview paper on the link between character education and attainment by Earl, S. and Arthur, J. here: https://www.jubileecentre.ac.uk/userfiles/jubileecentre/pdf/insight-series/Insight_Briefing_Paper_JA_SE.pdf.

[3] See, for example, Harrison, T., Dineen, K. and Moller, F. (2018), *Parent–Teachers Partnerships: Barriers and Enablers to Collaborative Character Education*, which can be downloaded here: https://www.jubileecentre.ac.uk/userfiles/jubileecentre/pdf/projects/TransformativeBritain/ParentTeacher_Partnerships.pdf.

[4] Peterson, C. and Seligman, M. (2004), *Character Strengths and Virtues*. Oxford: Oxford University Press.

[5] Dweck, C. (2017), *Mindset: The New Psychology of Success*. London, Robinson.

Chapter 18: Pedagogical Approaches to Developing Cyber-wisdom

[1] The caught, taught and sought distinction was first developed and outlined in the Jubilee Centre's *Framework for Character Education*. See https://www.jubileecentre.ac.uk/userfiles/jubileecentre/pdf/character-education/Framework%20for%20Character%20Education.pdf.

[2] These questions draw on the seven components of virtue that are outlined in the Jubilee Centre's *Framework for Character Education*. See https://www.jubileecentre.ac.uk/userfiles/jubileecentre/pdf/character-education/Framework%20for%20Character%20Education.pdf.

[3] See https://p4c.com/.

Chapter 19: Activities to Cultivate Cyber-wisdom

[1] See https://www.saferinternet.org.uk/.

[2] You can see the results of an evaluation of this programme in this paper: Harrison, T., Burn, E. and Moller, F. (2018), 'Teaching character: Cultivating virtue perception and virtue reasoning through the curriculum', *Educational Review*, 5, pp. 617–34.

Further Reading

Below, I suggest a few publications and resources on character, character education and the Internet that you might be interested in.

Books:

Shannon Vallor (2016), *Technology and the Virtues: A Philosophical Guide to a Future Worth Wanting*. One of the best books, underpinned by virtue ethics philosophy, that considers the impact that digital technology is having on individuals and on society.

Kristján Kristjánsson (2015), *Aristotelian Character Education*. Makes a convincing argument as to why character education should draw on neo-Aristotelian character-education theory.

James Arthur (2019), *The Formation of Character in Education: From Aristotle to the 21st Century*. A thought-provoking tour through the history of character education over the last two thousand years.

Carrie James (2014), *Disconnected: Youth, New Media and the Ethics Gap*. Looks closely at how young people think about the moral and ethical dilemmas they encounter when they share and use online content and participate in online communities.

Dean Cocking and Jeroen van den Hoven (2018), *Evil Online*. This book spells out, in no uncertain terms, the impact that online technologies are having on moral character.

Further advice on practice

Jubilee Centre for Character and Virtues

(www.jubileecentre.ac.uk). One of the world's foremost organisations researching character education. It also produces lots of free teaching resources. Look out in particular for the Framework for Character Education.

Common Sense Media (www.commonsensemedia.org). Its strapline is: *You know your kids. We know media and tech. Together we can build a digital world where our kids can thrive.* A great source of information for parents.

UK Safer Internet Centre (www.saferinternet.org.uk). An organisation that aims to promote the safe and responsible use of technology for young people. It offers training support and resources linked to Safer Internet Day.

Childnet (www.childnet.com). An international organisation offering free training for teachers and parents hoping to make the Internet a safe and great place for children.

Thinkuknow (www.thinkuknow.co.uk) is an education programme delivered by the National Crime Agency. The website offers advice, activities and support to protect children online and offline.

Acknowledgements

This book is the work of many. I typed the words, but they would never have come to me without the ideas and inspiration of my family, colleagues and friends.

The book is dedicated to my family: Emma, Isla and Sam. It is also inspired by them. I started the book because I was fascinated by how the ideas I had learnt during my studies would play out practically when my children started using the Internet. I want to thank Isla and Sam for allowing me to use them in this real-life experiment. I just hope I have fairly represented their joys, trials and tribulations of living in the age of the Internet. Emma has been a guide and sage throughout the time I have been writing the book (in fact the whole time I have known her) and many of the best bits here are thanks to her. She has helped me discover that the greatest of all human virtues are love, courage, wisdom and compassion – all of which she has in abundance.

On editing and revising the book, I was struck by how the wisdom of my mum and dad is represented in so much of what I have written. They showed, through their love, that who I am is more important than what I think and do. Without really mentioning it, they taught me that character mattered. My character was shaped (and occasionally tested!) by my brother and sister, whose wise thoughts are also represented in these pages. Growing up in my family has shaped me and it has shaped this book.

So many of the ideas here rest on what I have learnt from the colleagues I work with in the Jubilee Centre for Character and Virtues at the University of Birmingham. The Director of the Centre, James Arthur, has been the ideal mentor. He has offered equal amounts of encouragement and academic challenge – and knows instinctively exactly when each is needed and in what amount. The ideas about character and wisdom that the book rests upon draw heavily on the work of Kristján Kristjánsson (and, of course, his hero – Aristotle). Other colleagues in the Centre, including notably Andrew Peterson, Aidan Thompson, Danielle Edwards and Paul Watts, have helped me in many untold ways. Now is the moment for me to let past and present colleagues know how much they have taught me about what it means to flourish in the modern age.

Four colleagues in particular deserve a special mention for their direct involvement with the book. Thank you so much to Rachael Hunter who read several early drafts and put up with a great deal of unconstructed thoughts and some poor writing. Likewise, thank you David Laco for reading an almost final draft. I hope you can both see that many of your ideas have made it into the final version. Thank you also to Ben Millar and Matthew Collins for proofreading, editing and offering comments about the suitability of the educational activities I have included in the book.

Finally, I want to express a heartfelt thank you to my editor Tom Asker at Little, Brown Book Group. Tom was brave enough to take this book on. I found this out while sneakily checking emails on a cycling holiday with friends. My friends will tell you I punched the air when I found out. Over the last year, as I wrote the book, Tom has shown an abundance of character qualities including untold patience, good judgement, friendship, tolerance and a generosity of spirit. It has been a real pleasure to work with him. I am also enormously grateful to Nick Fawcett for his patient and careful copyediting of the manuscript, and to Rebecca Sheppard, of the Little, Brown Book Group, for all her work in preparing the book for production.

The people mentioned above and many others, including my friends, have been my most important real-life social network. You are a constant reminder that technologies only matter if they serve to make us more human.

Index